Simple Recipes to Spark the Spirit *of* Hospitality

Food That Says Welcome

Barbara Smith

Foreword by Gloria Gaither

WaterBrook Press

FOOD THAT SAYS WELCOME
PUBLISHED BY WATERBROOK PRESS
12265 Oracle Boulevard, Suite 200
Colorado Springs, Colorado 80921
A division of Random House, Inc.

10 Digit ISBN: 1-4000-7147-X
13 Digit ISBN: 978-1-4000-7147-0

Library of Congress Cataloging-in-Publication Data
Smith, Barbara.
Food that says welcome : simple recipes to spark the spirit of hospitality / Barbara Smith.—1st ed.
p. cm.
Includes index.
ISBN 1-4000-7147-X
1. Cookery, American. I. Title.
TX715.S651325 2006
641.5—dc22
2005026603

Printed in the United States of America
2006

10 9 8 7 6 5 4 3 2

I dedicate this book to all the women
who have been and are mentors in my life.
And my prayer for the reader is that you will be challenged
to create a lifestyle that says welcome
as you share life with others.

Contents

Foreword

I love it when Bill and I are seated in a restaurant next to a big, round table filled with a whole family—children, teenagers, parents, grandparents—eating together and engaged in eager conversation. I love it because I know parents can't make that easy, comfortable atmosphere of family interaction happen on the spur of the moment just to impress others in public. On the contrary, that comfortable kind of interchange comes from a habit of safe and joyful relationship cultivated over years of playing, working, and especially eating together as a family.

Psychologists tell us that eating together breaks down barriers. Physiologically, eating actually raises the body temperature, giving a feeling of warmth and comfort. Sitting around a table (and aren't round and oval tables the best?) puts us in a face-to-face position where we can not only hear the various contributions to the conversation but can also read the body language and facial expressions. No telling how many secrets have been told, knotty problems solved, and happy revelations shared around the kitchen table!

In every culture it seems the nurturing thing to do is to offer food or drink. A British mom is sure to say, "Here. What you need is a nice spot of tea," when she suspects her child, her friend, or her husband has had a rough day in the big, bad world.

For most of us Americans, warm cookies and milk will always bring back wonderful memories of coming in from school on a cold day. And is there anything as heartwarming as returning home after church to the aroma of a Sunday dinner of pot roast with potatoes, onions, and carrots simmering in the oven or smelling hot cider and popcorn on a winter's night?

I'm sure some Italians will argue that they can top those aromas with the smell of their family's spicy marinara sauce and crusty bread fresh from the oven.

The whole point is that it's impossible to separate memories, love, warmth, family, friends, and great hospitality from food. In *Food That Says Welcome,* Barbara Smith shares her family's secrets for not only the creation of great meals but also the *something more* that makes eating together such a life-forming experience.

It's not surprising that we have so many glimpses in the Bible of Jesus eating with His disciples. He had only three years to teach them, bind them together, and fortify them for what lay ahead. No wonder He often did it as He was broiling fish on a lakeside campfire, breaking bread in someone's house, or dividing up a picnic lunch so everyone would have plenty to share (with twelve basketfuls left over!). He wrapped His very mission in food.

If, as Barbara suggests, our mission as moms, hostesses, and hospitality givers is not only to feed the body but to nurture the soul, this is not just a cookbook. It is a way to wrap those at our table in wisdom, warmth, joy, and comfort at a time when our world so needs to come in from the cold and "break bread together."

—Gloria Gaither

Preface

My mother has been blessed with the gift of hospitality. I have watched her through the years prepare fabulous meals for our family and for hundreds of people, and she does so with such little effort. Her "prepare ahead of time" recipes allow her to enjoy spending time with her family and guests, and that is indeed an art. My girls, Mary Claire, Caroline, and Sarah Kate, are learning what hospitality means—and most of the lessons have come from their Mimi.

—Kimberly Smith Bennett

To welcome means to accept with pleasure the presence of another. To offer hospitality means to give a generous or cordial reception to guests, offering a pleasant or sustaining environment; it means sharing our lives in such a way that there is always room for one more. That is the concept of this cookbook—the enjoyment of sharing food and life with others. And I believe welcoming others with hospitality begins at home with friends and family.

It has been said that for every person you meet, you add a chapter to your life. My husband and I have been richly blessed with many wonderful "chapters" throughout our married years. I love people, and I am so thankful for our family and dear friends. The most important relationship to me, though, is my personal relationship with my heavenly Father. Out of my relationship with Him, God continues to place very special people in my life daily—my church family, my Sunday school class, my swim group, my prayer group, my Bible study group, the Room in the Inn ministry, my neighbors, and so many others.

In years past, many of our most precious memories with these loved ones have unfolded around the dinner table. The tradition of sharing good meals together continues today. We now have the privilege of remembering with long-term friends the special times of laughter, prayers, and support as we raised our families together. We also have the joy of building memories with friends old and new through the pleasure of dinnertime conversation.

Before I even began writing this cookbook, God opened the doors for me to share my beliefs about faith, family, and hospitality through speaking. When I talk with people at these engagements, I am reminded again and again that we all need a special place where we belong. As God's plan unfolds for me, I realize that many of us are enabled to create this special place in our home through a *lifestyle* that says, "Welcome." I always want to remember who we represent; we never know when we might be entertaining angels!

I am inspired by the mission statement of our church in Franklin, Tennessee: "To help transform ordinary people into passionate followers of Christ." Our pastor, Rick, continually challenges us to make a difference in the lives of others. His encouragement reminds me of one of my favorite verses from Galatians: "It is absolutely clear that God has called you to a free life. Just make sure that you don't use this freedom as an excuse to do whatever you want to do and destroy your freedom. Rather, use your freedom to serve one another in love; that's how freedom grows" (5:13, MSG).

My prayer is that this book will remind you of the freedom you have to serve others in love. The first priority for each of us is to have quiet time with our heavenly Father so that our lives are in order. Ask God daily for opportunities to serve others—and to discover the pleasure of extending mealtime beyond physical nourishment to something more.

Blessing

Dear heavenly Father,

We thank You and praise You and give You all the glory for the blessings You have so richly allowed us to experience—our relationship with You, our family, our friends, and those You place in our lives to serve. We thank You for this day and for the beauty of the earth and ask Your blessings on us as we seek Your wisdom, guidance, and direction in our daily lives. Bless this food, these friends, and our conversation. We pray this in Your precious name. Amen.

Acknowledgments

I want to thank my dear husband and best friend, Paul, for being such an encouragement to me while writing this book. He is also my taste tester! And a big thank-you to my family—Kimberly, David, Mary Claire, Caroline, and Sarah Kate; Michael, Debbie, Ryan, Whitney, Tyler, Anna, and Emily. I am eternally grateful to my heavenly Father for my precious family and friends and for the opportunities He has given me to serve Him.

I also want to thank Derek Jones and Don Pape for opening the door for this book and Shannon Hill, my editor, and Carol Bartley, production editor, and others at WaterBrook who have been so supportive in this project.

Very special thanks go to Gloria Gaither, Amy Grant, Joanne Kemp, Max Lucado, Shelley Breen, Jim Daneker, and Father Charles Stroebel for their special contribution to this book.

Introduction

Even though there are a lot of difficult things about being on the road as much as I am, one of the perks of my job is that I have had the good fortune to eat at some of the finest restaurants in the world. But you know what? I can honestly tell you that the best meals I've ever had—the ones that I've enjoyed the most—are those I've eaten at my mom's dinner table.

The food was always amazing, but when I think back over the years, I realize that what made those meals so wonderful was that my mom knew a secret. When Mom set the table, she wasn't just setting the table for eating—she was setting the table for conversation. She was setting the table for us to share, as a family, the ups and downs of our day. Mom was setting a place for us to spend an hour or more sitting and talking, enjoying each other, staying connected. This tradition has carried through to my wife, Debbie, and our family, and I know it continues for my sister, Kim, as well. At times now our families remain around the kitchen table long after the food is gone and the dishes have been cleared. I am so grateful to my parents for the lessons they taught me, and I'm especially thankful for the tradition that Mom created for us—all around a good meal.

I've heard it said that it's never too late to start a tradition. It's my hope that the recipes and stories that my mom has put together in this book will help you begin or continue the tradition of hospitality in your own family. You may find yourself at the table hours after the food has disappeared.

—Michael W. Smith

♡ Please note:

A heart before an ingredient means that a low-fat or light item could be substituted for it.

BEVERAGES

I was hungry and you gave me something to eat,
I was thirsty and you gave me something to drink,
I was a stranger and you invited me in.
—MATTHEW 25:35

The invitation to have a beverage is part of our greeting as we welcome friends and family into our home. The beverage choices are many, but the season usually influences what we offer.

Whether we are having guests or not, sweet tea is a favorite at the Smith home. Having eight granddaughters, we have been privileged to have many tea parties over the years. There is something special to the girls about pouring tea from the teapot and drinking tea from one of the china teacups I've collected.

The serving of beverages brings many special experiences to mind. Several years ago we were on a tour bus with Michael and his family going to Charlotte for a Billy Graham crusade. Michael wanted to stop and see Ruth Graham; she had been ill and had just returned from the hospital. We said we would stay on the bus while he and Debbie visited her, but Dr. Graham insisted that we all come in. Ruth was beautiful as she lay on her bed and welcomed each of us with a blessing. We were served beverages as we visited with Dr. Graham, his family, and the dogs. Then Ruth asked Michael to play "Amazing Grace" on the piano. This was a very special time for us, and it reminded me how we can always be gracious, even in illness.

More recently, God has placed me among twenty or so new friends in a wonderful Bible study group that includes women from a wide range of ages. Not only do these women inspire me with their bold desire to serve God, but I also appreciate how I am always welcomed with the offer of coffee, tea, and water—that simple but powerful invitation to love and fellowship.

Hospitality as ministry covers so many areas. We need to have an "open house" approach—to be available to meet the needs of others or to offer whatever help God lays on our hearts to provide.

Pineapple-Banana Punch

Yield: 40–50 (4-ounce) servings

4 bananas
1½ cups orange juice
2 cups sugar
1 (46-ounce) can pineapple juice
2 cups water
¼ cup lemon juice, fresh or bottled
3 quarts ginger ale

Mix bananas, orange juice, and sugar in blender and pour into large container. Add remaining ingredients except for ginger ale. Pour into 3 (1-quart) containers and freeze. When ready to serve, thaw 20 minutes and add 1 quart ginger ale to each quart punch base. Mix until slushy.

✎ **Grocery list:** bananas, orange juice, pineapple juice, ginger ale
✎ **Pantry checklist:** sugar, lemon juice

Hospitality Note: Keep the quart containers of punch base in your freezer for last-minute occasions.

Sherbet Punch

Yield: 36 (4-ounce) servings

1 (46-ounce) can pineapple juice
1 (6-ounce) can frozen lemonade
2 quarts ginger ale
1 quart lime sherbet

Mix juice and lemonade and add ginger ale and sherbet.

✎ **Grocery list:** pineapple juice, frozen lemonade, ginger ale, lime sherbet

Note: You can vary the kind of sherbet in this punch.

Favorite Strawberry Punch

Yield: 16 (4-ounce) servings

1 (12-ounce) can frozen lemonade
1 (10-ounce) package frozen strawberries
1 cup sugar
$1\frac{1}{2}$ cups water
1 quart ginger ale

Put lemonade, strawberries, and sugar in blender and mix well. Pour into bowl and add water. Mix well and freeze. Remove from freezer a half hour before serving and add ginger ale.

✎ **Grocery list:** frozen lemonade, frozen strawberries, ginger ale
✎ **Pantry checklist:** sugar

Yummy Breakfast Drink

Yield: 2 breakfast drinks

1 cup orange juice
♡8 ounces vanilla yogurt
1 frozen banana, sliced in chunks
4 fresh or frozen strawberries
sweetener or sugar to taste

Blend orange juice, yogurt, banana, strawberries, and sweetener together in blender.

✎ **Grocery list:** orange juice, vanilla yogurt, banana, strawberries
✎ **Pantry checklist:** sweetener or sugar

Hospitality Note: I keep frozen bananas and strawberries in the freezer for this quick morning drink.

WHITE GRAPE SPRITZER

Yield: 48 (4-ounce) servings

Easy, beautiful, and delicious!

1 (64-ounce) bottle white grape juice, chilled
4 quarts ginger ale, chilled
1 pint fresh strawberries, washed, with stems

Mix white grape juice with ginger ale just prior to serving. Place strawberries in punch bowl for garnish.

✎ **Grocery list:** white grape juice, ginger ale, fresh strawberries

Hospitality Note: Put an additional quart of ginger ale in a round Jell-O mold or in muffin tins. Add orange slices, fresh strawberries, washed holly leaves, or any fruit for color. Freeze. Tip out of container when frozen and float in punch bowl.

ORANGE SPRITZER

Yield: 24 (4-ounce) servings

2 quarts orange juice, chilled
1 quart ginger ale, chilled

Mix together just prior to serving. Garnish with fresh mint or a fresh orange slice.

✎ **Grocery list:** orange juice, ginger ale, fresh mint or orange

Hospitality Note: This is delicious served with brunch. You can freeze additional orange juice in ice-cube trays and serve with this spritzer instead of using ice cubes.

Cranberry and Orange Spritzer

Yield: 22 (4-ounce) servings

1 cup sugar
1 cup boiling water
4 cups cranberry juice, chilled
2 cups orange juice, chilled
3 cups club soda, chilled

Combine sugar and boiling water in a large container. Stir until sugar is dissolved. Cool and add cranberry juice and orange juice. Add club soda just prior to serving.

✎ **Grocery list:** cranberry juice, orange juice, club soda
✎ **Pantry checklist:** sugar

Hot Mocha Mix

Yield: 16 cups

1 cup nondairy coffee creamer
1/2 cup hot cocoa mix
1/2 cup instant coffee granules, finely ground
1 cup sugar
1 teaspoon cinnamon
1 teaspoon nutmeg

Mix all ingredients thoroughly. Store in covered container. To make 1 cup, spoon 3 tablespoons mix into mug or cup. Add 3/4 cup boiling water and stir until well blended.

✎ **Grocery list:** nondairy coffee creamer, hot cocoa mix, instant coffee
✎ **Pantry checklist:** sugar, cinnamon, nutmeg

Hospitality Note: This makes a great gift in decorated Mason jars! Give at Christmas or at any wintertime occasion where appropriate.

FRUIT-SPICED TEA

Yield: 10–12 (8-ounce) servings

2 family-sized tea bags
1 quart boiling water
2 cups sugar
1/2 cup Aspen Mulling Spices
1 (6-ounce) can frozen orange juice, thawed
1 (6-ounce) can frozen lemonade, thawed
1 1/2 cups cold water
1 quart ginger ale
mint leaves or sliced lemon, for garnish

Steep tea bags in boiling water for 5–7 minutes. Remove tea bags; add sugar and mulling spices, stirring to dissolve. Place sweetened tea in very large container and add orange juice, lemonade, and water. Just prior to serving, add ginger ale. Garnish with fresh mint leaves or sliced lemon.

✎ **Grocery list:** tea bags, Aspen Mulling Spices, orange juice, lemonade, ginger ale, fresh mint or lemons

✎ **Pantry checklist:** sugar

CHRISTMAS FRUIT TEA

Yield: 50 (4-ounce) servings

2 family-sized tea bags
2 cups boiling water
1 cup sugar
1/2 cup Aspen Mulling Spices
3 cups pineapple juice
4 cups lemonade
4 cups orange juice
4 cups cranberry juice
4 cups apple juice
1 (1-liter) bottle ginger ale

Steep tea bags in boiling water for several minutes. Remove tea bags and stir in sugar and mulling spices until mixture is dissolved. Combine juices, lemonade, and tea mixture in a large container and chill. Add ginger ale when ready to serve.

✎ **Grocery list:** tea bags, Aspen Mulling Spices, pineapple juice, lemonade, orange juice, cranberry juice, apple juice, ginger ale

✎ **Pantry checklist:** sugar

Wassail

Yield: 25 (4-ounce) servings

2 quarts apple juice
2 cups pineapple juice
2 cups orange juice
1/2 cup fresh lemon juice
1/2 cup sugar
1 (3-inch) stick cinnamon
1 teaspoon whole cloves

Combine all ingredients in a large pan and bring to a boil. Then reduce heat and simmer 20 minutes, covered. Uncover and simmer an additional 20 minutes. Strain. Discard cinnamon and cloves. Serve hot.

✎ **Grocery list:** apple juice, pineapple juice, orange juice, lemon juice

✎ **Pantry checklist:** sugar, stick cinnamon, whole cloves

Easy Wassail

Yield: 20 (4-ounce) servings

A delicious and easy variation!

64 ounces apple juice
16 ounces ginger ale
1/2 cup Aspen Mulling Spices

Mix together in a large pan and heat thoroughly.

✎ **Grocery list:** apple juice, ginger ale, Aspen Mulling Spices

APPETIZERS

Therefore, as we have opportunity, let us do good to all people,
especially to those who belong to the family of believers.
—GALATIANS 6:10

A wonderful "welcome food," appetizers offer a great way for guests to become acquainted and visit with each other as they gather around the serving area at open houses, parties, and other occasions.

Each time my son, Michael, begins rehearsing for tour, I prepare and take appetizers to the rehearsal hall for the band. They each have favorites that I make for them, but this also gives me an opportunity to try out new recipes. Appetizers are definitely a welcome food—a great way for us to meet new people and visit with them. For the last several years Point of Grace and the Katinas have been part of Michael's Christmas tour. They have become my extended "music family." I also appreciate all the people backstage—Joey, Shane, and the many others who make the concerts and travel go smoothly. They are the unsung heroes. These are wonderful and talented young people whom I love and care about.

We occasionally host an open house at our home; this

gives us a great opportunity to meet new friends and get better acquainted with others. Appetizers are the standard fare for these nights, and I prepare many of them in advance so I will have plenty of time with our guests.

> Food and family—two of life's greatest blessings! It's strangely magical that the simple smell of Mom's kitchen can evoke such strong feelings of comfort. Everything I know about cooking, entertaining, and serving others, I learned by example. There is, quite simply, nothing more fulfilling than sharing your heart, home, and food with the people you love.
>
> —Shelley Breen, Point of Grace

> Some of my best memories of working with Michael over the years are the times we've spent behind the scenes getting ready to hit the road. Just about every time we rehearse, Michael's parents come walking in with *multiple* loads of food, and of course the band makes a beeline for Barbara's irresistible cinnamon rolls!
>
> What really stands out even more than the food (if that's possible) is the graciousness and servant hearts that Barbara and Paul model. They simply make everyone feel like family—*their* family, and that's such a blessing to be around. My wife and I strive to give those same gifts of hospitality, welcome, and friendship to people who visit our home. Thanks for the great example, Barbara and Paul!
>
> —Jim Daneker, keyboardist/programmer,
> Michael W. Smith Band

Easy Salsa Picante

Yield: 4 cups

1 cup coarsely chopped onion
1/2 cup cilantro
1 jalapeño pepper, coarsely chopped
1 clove garlic, chopped
1 (14 1/2-ounce) can diced tomatoes, undrained
3 tablespoons fresh lime juice
1/2 teaspoon salt (or more for taste)
1 (14 1/2-ounce) can petite diced tomatoes, drained
♡chips, to serve

Mix first 5 ingredients in food processor and process until minced. Combine this mixture with lime juice, salt, and drained petite tomatoes.

✎ **Grocery list:** cilantro, jalapeño pepper, diced tomatoes, lime, petite diced tomatoes, chips

✎ **Pantry checklist:** onion, garlic, salt

Black Bean Salsa

Yield: 10–12 servings

2 (10-ounce) cans petite diced tomatoes with green chilies, drained
2 (11-ounce) cans yellow sweet corn, drained
2 (15 1/2-ounce) cans black beans, rinsed and drained
1 purple onion, diced
2 tablespoons fresh lime juice
♡3 tablespoons olive oil
fresh chopped cilantro to taste
salt and pepper to taste
♡chips, to serve

Mix together and serve with chips.

✎ **Grocery list:** petite diced tomatoes with green chilies, yellow sweet corn, black beans, purple onion, lime, cilantro, chips

✎ **Pantry checklist:** olive oil, salt, pepper

Smitty's Favorite Salsa

Yield: 8 cups

1/4 cup red pepper, cut into large pieces
1/2 green pepper, chopped
1 jalapeño pepper, chopped
1/2 cup onion, cut into large pieces
1 (4 1/2-ounce) can chopped green chilies, drained
1/2 cup fresh cilantro, chopped (use amount according to your taste)
2 (29-ounce) cans crushed tomatoes
1 teaspoon sugar
2 tablespoons fresh lime juice
salt and pepper to taste
♡chips, to serve

Mix first 5 ingredients in food processor and pulse until finely chopped. Add cilantro and chop again. Remove from processor and add remaining ingredients.

✎ **Grocery list:** red pepper, green pepper, jalapeño pepper, green chilies, cilantro, crushed tomatoes, lime, chips

✎ **Pantry checklist:** onion, sugar, salt, pepper

Fresh Cilantro Salsa

Yield: 12+ servings

2 (14 1/2-ounce) cans Mexican-style stewed tomatoes
1 or 2 (4 1/2-ounce) cans chopped green chilies, drained (depending on your taste)
1 (8-ounce) can tomato sauce
1/2 cup chopped purple onion
1 clove garlic, minced
1 bunch fresh cilantro, chopped (use quantity according to your taste)
♡1 tablespoon olive oil
♡chips, to serve

Pulse all ingredients together in food processor to desired consistency.

✎ **Grocery list:** Mexican-style stewed tomatoes, green chilies, tomato sauce, purple onion, cilantro, chips

✎ **Pantry checklist:** garlic, olive oil

HOT BLACK BEAN DIP

Yield: 6 servings

♡*1 pound ground chuck, cooked and crumbled*
1 package taco seasoning mix
2 (15-ounce) cans black beans, drained
1 (16-ounce) jar salsa or picante sauce
♡*2 cups shredded mozzarella cheese*
♡*sour cream and tortilla chips, to serve*

Preheat oven to 350 degrees.

Mix ground chuck with taco seasoning and spoon into 2-quart baking dish. Layer with beans and then salsa, and top with cheese. Bake 15–20 minutes or until hot. Serve with chips and sour cream.

✎ **Grocery list:** ground chuck, taco seasoning mix, black beans, salsa or picante sauce, mozzarella cheese, sour cream, tortilla chips

HOT SPINACH DIP

Yield: 4 cups

1 (10-ounce) package frozen chopped spinach, thawed and drained
♡*1 (8-ounce) package cream cheese, room temperature*
♡*1 cup shredded Monterey Jack cheese*
1/2 cup freshly grated Parmesan cheese
1/2 small onion, chopped
1 (14-oz) can artichoke hearts, drained and chopped
1 (10-ounce) can diced tomatoes with green chilies, drained
1 teaspoon cumin
1 teaspoon chili powder
1 clove garlic, minced
toasted pita chips, to serve

Preheat oven to 350 degrees.

Press spinach between layers of paper towels to remove excess moisture. Mix spinach and cream cheese well, then add remaining ingredients. Place mixture in a greased 9-x-13-inch glass baking dish and bake 30 minutes. Serve with toasted pita chips.

✎ **Grocery list:** frozen chopped spinach, cream cheese, Monterey Jack cheese, Parmesan cheese, artichoke hearts, diced tomatoes with green chilies, toasted pita chips

✎ **Pantry checklist:** onion, cumin, chili powder, garlic

Spinach-Artichoke Dip

Yield: 8 servings

1 (10-ounce) package frozen chopped spinach
1 (14-ounce) can artichoke hearts, drained and chopped
♡*1 cup shredded Monterey Jack or mozzarella cheese*
♡*4 ounces cream cheese, room temperature*
1 cup freshly grated Parmesan cheese
♡*1/2 cup mayonnaise*
1 clove garlic, minced
1/2 teaspoon cayenne
1 teaspoon Worcestershire sauce
♡*tortilla chips, pita chips, or crackers, to serve*

Preheat oven to 350 degrees.

Thaw spinach for 3 1/2 minutes in the microwave on high and then drain well. Mix artichokes, spinach, Monterey Jack or mozzarella cheese, cream cheese, Parmesan cheese, mayonnaise, garlic, cayenne, and Worcestershire sauce together and spoon into a lightly greased 1-quart casserole dish. Bake 20–30 minutes. Serve warm with tortilla chips, pita chips, or crackers.

✎ **Grocery list:** frozen chopped spinach, artichoke hearts, Monterey Jack or mozzarella cheese, cream cheese, Parmesan cheese, chips or crackers
✎ **Pantry checklist:** mayonnaise, garlic, cayenne, Worcestershire sauce

Cocktail Sauce

Yield: 3 cups

1 (12-ounce) bottle chili sauce
4 tablespoons prepared horseradish
1 cup ketchup
juice of 2 lemons plus equal amount of sugar
shrimp, to serve

Mix together and chill. Serve with fresh shrimp.

✎ **Grocery list:** chili sauce, horseradish, lemons, shrimp
✎ **Pantry checklist:** ketchup, sugar

Tomato-Cheddar Cheese Spread

Yield: 3 cups

1 (10-ounce) can diced tomatoes with green chilies, drained
♡1 cup mayonnaise
1 teaspoon Worcestershire sauce
♡2 (8-ounce) blocks sharp cheddar cheese, shredded
1 (4-ounce) jar diced pimiento, well drained
♡crackers or chips, to serve

Mix all ingredients together and chill. Serve with crackers or chips.

✎ **Grocery list:** diced tomatoes with green chilies, sharp cheddar cheese, pimientos, crackers or chips

✎ **Pantry checklist:** mayonnaise, Worcestershire sauce

Pimiento Cheese

Yield: 5 cups

♡4 cups shredded sharp cheddar cheese
1/2–3/4 cup diced pimiento, drained
1 packet sweetener
♡3/4 cup mayonnaise (or more, depending on the consistency you want)
♡crackers, chips, or celery, to serve

Blend ingredients together. (I prefer using a food processor for this recipe.) Store in refrigerator.

Serve with crackers, chips, or celery.

✎ **Grocery list:** sharp cheddar cheese; pimientos; crackers, chips, or celery

✎ **Pantry checklist:** sweetener, mayonnaise

Apples with Cream Cheese Dip

Yield: 20 servings

♡1 *(8-ounce) package cream cheese, room temperature*
1/4 *cup powdered sugar (or artificial sweetener)*
1 *jar caramel sauce*
1/2 *cup finely chopped pecans or walnuts, toasted*
2 *Red Delicious apples, unpeeled and sliced*
2 *Granny Smith apples, unpeeled and sliced*
1/2 *cup ginger ale*

Mix cream cheese and sugar thoroughly. Mold in center of plate and drizzle caramel sauce on top. Sprinkle with pecans or walnuts. Wash and slice apples, then dip in ginger ale to keep from turning brown. Alternate red and green slices around edge of the dish. Delicious!

✎ **Grocery list:** cream cheese, powdered sugar, caramel sauce, pecans or walnuts, Red Delicious apples, Granny Smith apples, ginger ale

Tropical Cream Cheese Spread

Yield: 1 1/2 cups

♡1 *(8-ounce) package cream cheese, room temperature*
3 *tablespoons apricot preserves*
1/3 *cup crushed pineapple, drained*
2 *teaspoons honey*
fresh fruit or gingersnaps, to serve

Combine ingredients in food processor until smooth. Refrigerate until ready to serve. Serve with fresh fruit or gingersnaps.

✎ **Grocery list:** cream cheese, apricot preserves, crushed pineapple, fruit or gingersnaps
✎ **Pantry checklist:** honey

FRUITED CHEESE TORTE

Yield: 12 servings

♡2 *(8-ounce) packages cream cheese, room temperature and divided*
1/2 *cup crushed pineapple, well drained*
1/2 *cup apricot preserves*
1 *cup pecans, chopped and toasted*
♡1/2 *cup shredded sharp cheddar cheese*
1/4 *cup raspberry hot jelly*
1/2 *cup roasted raspberry chipotle sauce*
♡*crackers, to serve*

In a small bowl, beat 8 ounces of cream cheese until smooth; add pineapple and apricot preserves. Line a 6-inch bowl with plastic wrap. Spread cream cheese mixture into bowl and top with toasted pecans. Mix remaining cream cheese with cheddar cheese and spread on top of pecans. Cover and refrigerate overnight. When ready to serve, remove cheese torte to serving dish. Mix the raspberry hot jelly and chipotle sauce together and spread over cheese. Serve with crackers.

✎ **Grocery list:** cream cheese, crushed pineapple, apricot preserves, pecans, sharp cheddar cheese, hot raspberry jelly, roasted raspberry chipotle sauce (Note: You'll find the jelly and chipotle sauce in the specialty section of the grocery store.)

BACON-CHEESE SQUARES

Yield: 20+ bread squares

♡1 *cup shredded Swiss cheese*
1 *green onion, chopped*
♡8 *slices bacon, cooked crisp and crumbled*
♡3–4 *tablespoons mayonnaise*
2 *tablespoons diced pimiento, drained*
1 *loaf of sliced party rye bread*

Preheat oven to 350 degrees.

Mix Swiss cheese, green onion, bacon, mayonnaise, and pimiento, and spread on party rye bread. Bake 10 minutes.

✎ **Grocery list:** Swiss cheese, green onions, bacon, pimientos, party rye bread
✎ **Pantry checklist:** mayonnaise

Hospitality Note: These can be put together in advance and frozen. Bake when ready to serve.

Mexican Cheese Ball

Yield: 8 servings

♡2 (8-ounce) packages cream cheese, room temperature
3 green onions, chopped
♡1/2 cup shredded cheddar cheese
3 tablespoons taco seasoning
1/4 cup salsa
1/8 teaspoon salt
2 tablespoons chopped fresh parsley
1 cup chopped pecans, toasted
♡crackers, to serve

Mix cream cheese, green onions, cheddar cheese, taco seasoning, salsa, salt, and parsley together and form into 2 small balls. Chill cheese balls and then roll in toasted pecans. Serve with crackers.

✎ **Grocery list:** cream cheese, green onions, cheddar cheese, taco seasoning, salsa, pecans, crackers

✎ **Pantry checklist:** salt, parsley

Hospitality Note: Dividing the mixture into two cheese balls allows you to serve one and then, when it is nearly eaten, to replace it with a fresh cheese ball.

ASPARAGUS ROLLS

Yield: 30 rolls

30 slices wheat berry bread or bread of your choice
2 (8-ounce) containers herbed cream cheese, room temperature
1/4 cup freshly grated Parmesan cheese
1/4 teaspoon seasoning salt
♡*1/4 cup mayonnaise*
1 can asparagus spears, drained
1/4 cup butter, melted
paprika

Preheat oven to 375 degrees.

Remove crust from bread and use a rolling pin to flatten each slice of bread. Combine herbed cream cheese, Parmesan cheese, seasoning salt, and mayonnaise, mixing well. Spread cheese mixture on bread, covering well. Lay 1 asparagus spear on each slice of bread and roll up; place seam side down on a greased baking sheet. Brush each roll with butter and sprinkle with paprika. Bake 10–12 minutes.

✎ **Grocery list:** bread, herbed cream cheese, Parmesan cheese, asparagus
✎ **Pantry checklist:** seasoning salt, mayonnaise, butter, paprika

Hospitality Note: These can be prepared in advance and frozen. Bake just prior to serving.

Southwestern Tart

Yield: 6 servings

1 refrigerated piecrust
♡1 (8-ounce) package cream cheese, room temperature
2 eggs
2 green onions, chopped
1/2 teaspoon cumin
2 tablespoons fresh cilantro, chopped
1/4 teaspoon salt
1 ripe avocado, chopped
2 tablespoons fresh lime juice
♡1/2 cup sour cream
♡1/2 cup shredded cheddar cheese
2 Roma tomatoes, chopped
♡salsa and chips, to serve

Preheat oven to 400 degrees.

Roll piecrust to fit 9-inch tart pan. Bake 5 minutes. Cool.

Beat cream cheese at medium speed in mixer until smooth. Add eggs, green onions, cumin, cilantro, and salt and mix well. Spread evenly over crust. Bake 20 minutes, then cool for 10 minutes. Toss avocado with lime juice. Spread sour cream over egg mixture in piecrust. Sprinkle with cheddar cheese and avocado and top with chopped tomatoes. Serve with salsa and chips.

✎ **Grocery list:** piecrust, cream cheese, green onions, fresh cilantro, avocado, lime, sour cream, cheddar cheese, Roma tomatoes, salsa, chips
✎ **Pantry checklist:** eggs, cumin, salt

Crab Dip

Yield: 3 cups

8 ounces fresh crabmeat
♡1 (8-ounce) container sour cream
♡1 (8-ounce) package cream cheese, room temperature
1 green onion, sliced
dash of paprika
♡crackers or pita chips, to serve

Mix all ingredients well and chill. Serve with crackers or pita chips.

Grocery list: fresh crabmeat, sour cream, cream cheese, green onions, crackers or pita chips
Pantry checklist: paprika

Chicken Fingers with Honey-Horseradish Dip

Yield: 16 tenderloins

♡*16 saltine crackers, finely crushed*
1/4 cup pecans, toasted and ground
1/2 teaspoon salt
1/2 teaspoon pepper
2 teaspoons paprika
1 egg white
16 chicken tenderloins

Preheat oven to 400 degrees.

Stir together first 5 ingredients.

Whisk egg white until frothy; dip chicken tenderloins into egg white and dredge in saltine mixture. Place chicken tenderloins on well-greased baking sheet. Bake 18–20 minutes or until golden brown.

Honey-Horseradish Dip

♡*1/2 cup sour cream*
1/4 cup Dijon mustard
1/4 cup honey
2 tablespoons prepared horseradish

Mix ingredients together and serve with chicken.

✎ **Grocery list:** saltine crackers, pecans, chicken tenderloins, sour cream, horseradish

✎ **Pantry checklist:** salt, pepper, paprika, egg, Dijon mustard, honey

Pineapple Cheese Ball

Yield: 2 cheese balls

♡*2 (8-ounce) packages cream cheese, room temperature*
2 teaspoons minced onion
1 (8 1/2-ounce) can crushed pineapple, drained
1/4 cup green pepper, finely chopped
1 teaspoon seasoned salt
2 cups pecans, finely chopped, toasted
♡*crackers or celery, to serve*

Mix first 5 ingredients together. Chill and shape into 2 cheese balls and roll in pecans.

✎ **Grocery list:** cream cheese, crushed pineapple, green pepper, pecans, crackers or celery

✎ **Pantry checklist:** onion, seasoned salt

Chicken Salad Puffs

Yield: 50 puffs

1/2 cup butter
1 cup boiling water
1 cup flour
1/4 teaspoon salt
4 eggs

Preheat oven to 400 degrees.

Melt butter in boiling water; add flour and salt, stirring vigorously until mixture forms a ball. Remove from heat and cool slightly. Add eggs 1 at a time, mixing well after each addition until eggs are absorbed.

Using a teaspoon, form pastry into small balls and place on ungreased nonstick baking sheet. Bake for 15 minutes, then reduce temperature to 325 degrees and bake 15–20 minutes more or until pastries have browned. Cool on wire rack.

Fill with chicken salad (recipe on page 82) or pimiento cheese (recipe on page 17).

✎ **Pantry checklist:** butter, flour, salt, eggs

> ***Hospitality Note:*** The puffs may be made a couple of days prior to serving; store in cool area. Fill just before serving.

Sesame Chicken

Yield: 24 tenderloins

24 chicken tenderloins

Marinade

♡ *1 1/2 cups buttermilk*
2 tablespoons lemon juice
1 teaspoon soy sauce
1 teaspoon paprika
1 tablespoon Italian seasoning
1 teaspoon salt
1 teaspoon pepper
2 cloves garlic, minced

Breadcrumb Topping

1/4 cup butter, melted
1/4 cup shortening, melted
4 cups soft breadcrumbs
1/2 cup sesame seeds
sweet-and-sour sauce, honey mustard dressing, or cocktail sauce, to serve

Preheat oven to 375 degrees.

Place chicken tenderloins in dish with a tight-fitting lid.

Mix marinade ingredients together well and pour over chicken. Cover and refrigerate 6–8 hours to marinate.

When ready to bake, drain chicken. Melt butter and shortening together. Roll tenderloins in breadcrumbs and place on well-greased, large cooking sheet. Pour butter-shortening mix over tenderloins and sprinkle with sesame seeds. Bake 30 minutes until well browned. Serve with sweet-and-sour sauce, honey mustard dressing, or cocktail sauce (see page 16).

✎ **Grocery list:** chicken tenderloins, buttermilk, sesame seeds, sweet-and-sour sauce or cocktail sauce

✎ **Pantry checklist:** lemon juice, soy sauce, paprika, Italian seasoning, salt, pepper, garlic, butter, shortening, breadcrumbs

MINI TACOS

Yield: 80 or more tacos

This is a favorite of many, but most of all my grandchildren.

1 (1-pound) package egg-roll wrappers
♡*1 pound ground chuck, cooked, drained, and crumbled*
1 package taco seasoning mix
1 (16-ounce) jar salsa
♡*1 (16-ounce) package finely shredded cheddar cheese*
♡*1 (8-ounce) container sour cream*

Preheat oven to 350 degrees.

Remove wrappers from refrigerator 30 minutes before cutting them.

With scissors, cut egg-roll wrappers across twice, horizontally and vertically to make 9 stacks. Then trim off edges. Place wrappers in miniature muffin pans and bake for 5 minutes or until browned. (Note: They brown quickly.)

Mix ground chuck with taco seasoning and salsa. Serve meat mixture in chafing dish, with the taco shells, cheese, and sour cream in bowls on the side.

✎ **Grocery list:** egg-roll wrappers (produce section), ground chuck, taco seasoning mix, salsa, cheddar cheese, sour cream

Hospitality Note: The baked wrappers can be stored for a month in a closed container, or you can freeze them for several months. The meat for this dish can also be prepared in advance and frozen until ready for use.

DEEP-DISH TACO PIZZA

Yield: 6 servings

♡*1 pound ground chuck*
1/2 cup chopped onion
1 teaspoon taco seasoning mix
1 (15-ounce) can diced tomatoes with green chilies, drained
1 (10-ounce) package refrigerated pizza-crust dough
♡*1/2 cup shredded cheddar cheese*
♡*1/2 cup shredded mozzarella cheese*
♡*sour cream and salsa, to serve*

Preheat oven to 400 degrees.

Cook beef and onion in a large skillet until well done. Drain the ground meat and rinse with water to remove excess fat. (For a finer texture, place meat in a food processor and pulse for a few seconds.) Return to the skillet and stir in taco seasoning mix and tomatoes. Cook until thoroughly heated.

Meanwhile, unroll pizza dough and press onto bottom and up the sides of a lightly greased 9-x-13-inch glass baking dish. Spoon meat mixture over crust and bake 10–12 minutes. Remove from oven and top with cheeses. Bake 5 more minutes until cheese is melted and crust has browned. Serve with salsa and sour cream.

✎ **Grocery list:** ground chuck, taco seasoning mix, diced tomatoes with green chilies, refrigerated pizza-crust dough, cheddar cheese, mozzarella cheese, sour cream, salsa

✎ **Pantry checklist:** onion

Won Ton Cups

Yield: 3 dozen

1 pound cooked sausage, crumbled and well drained
♡1½ cups shredded cheddar cheese
♡1½ cups shredded Monterey Jack cheese
½ cup diced pimiento, drained
¼ cup green chilies, chopped and drained (optional)
♡¾ cup ranch dressing
¼ cup chopped fresh parsley
1 package won ton wrappers

Preheat oven to 350 degrees.

Mix first 7 ingredients well in a bowl and set aside.

Place won ton wrappers in miniature muffin tins. Bake 3–4 minutes or until lightly brown. Remove from oven and fill with sausage mixture. Bake 6–8 minutes or until hot and browned.

✎ **Grocery list:** sausage, cheddar cheese, Monterey Jack cheese, pimientos, green chilies, ranch dressing, parsley, won ton wrappers

Hospitality Note: This appetizer can be prepared in advance. Bake won ton wrappers, put them in a container with a lid, and store in a cool place or freeze. Also, the filling can be put together in advance and frozen. Time savers!

BEEF TENDERLOIN WITH HORSERADISH SAUCE

Yield: 20+ servings

1 whole beef tenderloin, trimmed

Marinade

1 cup pineapple juice
1 teaspoon ginger
2 cloves garlic, minced
♡1/3 cup soy sauce
1 teaspoon sugar
♡1/3 cup olive oil

Preheat oven to 400 degrees.

Mix marinade ingredients together and pour over the tenderloin. Cover and marinate the tenderloin overnight in refrigerator. Prior to baking, drain. Bake on well-greased baking sheet 45–60 minutes, depending on how well done you like your meat. Cover with foil and cool 15 minutes before slicing for rolls.

Horseradish Sauce

♡1 (8-ounce) container sour cream
♡1/2 cup mayonnaise
1 tablespoon Dijon mustard
2 tablespoons fresh parsley or basil
4 teaspoons horseradish
1 clove garlic, minced
rolls, to serve

Mix all ingredients.

Serve sliced tenderloin on rolls with horseradish sauce.

✎ **Grocery list:** beef tenderloin, pineapple juice, sour cream, fresh parsley or basil, horseradish, rolls

✎ **Pantry checklist:** ginger, garlic, soy sauce, sugar, olive oil, mayonnaise, Dijon mustard

Hospitality Note: You can keep fresh marinade in the refrigerator for later use. It is delicious on pork, chicken, or beef.

Pork Tenderloin Rolls

Yield: 50 small rolls

1/4 cup honey
2 tablespoons apple cider vinegar
1 tablespoon Dijon mustard
1/2 teaspoon paprika
2 pork tenderloins

Preheat oven to 350 degrees.

Combine honey, vinegar, mustard, and paprika. Place tenderloins in lightly greased pan. Cover tenderloins with honey mixture. Bake 40 minutes. Cool and slice.

Rolls

1 package dry yeast
1 teaspoon and 1/2 cup sugar, divided
1/2 cup warm water
1/2 cup shortening
1/2 cup boiling water
1/2 cup cold water
1 egg, beaten
1 teaspoon salt
3 cups flour
♡honey mustard dressing

Preheat oven to 375 degrees.

Cover yeast and 1 teaspoon sugar with 1/2 cup warm water; let set for 5 minutes or until it bubbles. In a separate bowl, combine remaining sugar and shortening and blend well. Pour boiling water over the shortening mixture and stir until melted. Add 1/2 cup cold water, yeast mixture, egg, salt, and flour and mix well. Refrigerate overnight or at least 2 hours. Roll dough out on floured surface; cut with small biscuit cutter and place on greased baking sheet. Let rise until doubled (about 1 hour). Bake 10–12 minutes or until browned. Slice rolls, spread with honey mustard dressing, and fill with sliced pork tenderloin.

✎ **Grocery list:** pork tenderloins, dry yeast, honey mustard dressing

✎ **Pantry checklist:** honey, apple cider vinegar, Dijon mustard, paprika, sugar, shortening, egg, salt, flour

Note: You can substitute 2 pounds of deli ham for the pork tenderloin. When using ham, spread the rolls with honey mustard dressing and mayonnaise.

BREADS

I am the bread of life. He who comes to me will never go hungry,
and he who believes in me will never be thirsty.
—JOHN 6:35

This is the category I have had the most experience with. Sometimes I wonder how many bags of flour I have bought in my life, how many rolls I have formed, and how many biscuits and muffins I have shared with others. My grandchildren love bread and strawberry preserves. I must admit, this category is also my personal favorite. I would rather have bread than dessert!

Bread making is an example of a craft that has been lost to modern conveniences. It's easy to get fresh bread from bread machines or gourmet stores, but the value of bread is lessened when you don't have to put much effort into making it.

When you are making bread, you can use part of the dough to create sweet rolls of different varieties and then freeze the rolls for another occasion or a gift. Bread itself makes a great gift. It is a way for me to respond to those who care about my family and me. For example, I am always inspired by two doctor friends who are now in health-related services. They still carry their black bags and spend their time off caring and praying for those who need them. Their hearts and ministry are in service to others. These friends have come to our home on a Sunday afternoon to care for us, and one of the best ways I know to thank them is with the gift of homemade bread.

I still bake homemade bread every week, not for Paul and me, but for the other occasions that arise—opportunities to give to the homeless, the sick, the bereaved, or the grandkids, who love it! Because bread takes hours to make, it expresses a love that only time invested in hospitality can convey. It is a simple pleasure. Offering homemade bread as a gift is a beautiful way to care for someone else.

BUTTERMILK BISCUITS

Yield: 10–12 biscuits

2 cups flour
1 tablespoon baking powder
2 teaspoons sugar
1/2 teaspoon cream of tartar
1/4 teaspoon salt
1/4 teaspoon baking soda
1/2 cup shortening
♡*2/3 cup buttermilk*

Preheat oven to 450 degrees.

In a medium bowl, stir together flour, baking powder, sugar, cream of tartar, salt, and baking soda. Using a pastry blender, cut in shortening until mixture resembles coarse crumbs. Make a well in center and add buttermilk, stirring just until moistened.

Turn dough out onto lightly floured surface and knead gently. Pat or roll dough to 1/2-inch thickness. Cut with biscuit cutter dipped in flour. Place biscuits on well-greased cookie sheet and bake 10–12 minutes or until browned.

✎ **Grocery list:** buttermilk

✎ **Pantry checklist:** flour, baking powder, sugar, cream of tartar, salt, baking soda, shortening

Carrot-Pineapple Cupcakes

Yield: 18 cupcakes

1 cup flour
1 cup sugar
1 teaspoon baking soda
1 teaspoon cinnamon
1 teaspoon ginger
1 teaspoon nutmeg
1/2 teaspoon salt
1/2 cup vegetable oil
1/4 cup butter, melted
1 teaspoon vanilla
2 eggs
1 1/2 cups grated carrots
1/2 cup crushed pineapple, drained
1/2 cup raisins
1/2 cup chopped walnuts

Preheat oven to 350 degrees.

Blend flour, sugar, baking soda, cinnamon, ginger, nutmeg, and salt in a large bowl. In a separate bowl, whisk oil, butter, vanilla, and eggs together well. Spoon into flour mixture and blend. Add carrots, pineapple, raisins, and walnuts and mix. Spoon into lined muffin tins and bake 20–25 minutes or until done. Cool in pans 10 minutes before removing.

Frosting

♡*1 (8-ounce) package cream cheese, room temperature*
1/4 cup butter, softened
1 teaspoon vanilla
2 1/2–3 cups powdered sugar (depending on desired consistency)

Mix all ingredients together and frost cupcakes.

✎ **Grocery list:** carrots, crushed pineapple, raisins, walnuts, cream cheese, powdered sugar

✎ **Pantry checklist:** flour, sugar, baking soda, cinnamon, ginger, nutmeg, salt, vegetable oil, butter, vanilla, eggs

CRANBERRY STREUSEL MUFFINS

Yield: 18 muffins

2 cups flour, divided
1 cup firmly packed brown sugar
1/2 cup butter, room temperature
2/3 cup walnuts, chopped and divided
2 teaspoons baking powder
1/2 teaspoon baking soda
1/2 teaspoon salt
1 teaspoon nutmeg
2 large eggs, lightly beaten
♡*1/3 cup buttermilk*
♡*1/3 cup sour cream*
1 cup fresh cranberries, coarsely chopped

Preheat oven to 350 degrees.

Combine 1 cup flour and brown sugar; cut in butter with pastry blender until mixture is crumbly. Place half of this mixture in a small bowl and mix with 3 tablespoons chopped walnuts. Set aside.

Combine remaining flour-sugar-butter mixture with 1 cup flour, baking powder, baking soda, salt, and nutmeg. In a separate bowl, combine eggs, buttermilk, and sour cream. Add to the flour mixture that includes the baking powder, stirring just until moistened. Stir in cranberries and remaining walnuts. Spoon into greased muffin tins and top with flour-sugar-butter mixture. Bake 20 minutes or until done. Cool in pans 10 minutes before removing.

✎ **Grocery list:** walnuts, buttermilk, sour cream, cranberries

✎ **Pantry checklist:** flour, brown sugar, butter, baking powder, baking soda, salt, nutmeg, eggs

Morning Glory Muffins

Yield: 2 dozen muffins

2 1/2 cups flour
1 1/4 cups sugar
2 teaspoons cinnamon
1 teaspoon nutmeg
2 teaspoons baking soda
1/2 teaspoon salt
3 eggs
3/4 cup applesauce
1/2 cup vegetable oil
1 teaspoon vanilla
2 cups grated carrots
1 Granny Smith apple, peeled and grated
1 cup crushed pineapple, drained
1/2 cup raisins
1/2 cup chopped walnuts

Preheat oven to 350 degrees.

Combine the first 6 ingredients in a large bowl. In another bowl, combine the eggs, applesauce, oil, and vanilla. Stir into dry ingredients just until moistened. Stir in remaining ingredients. Fill greased muffin tins 2/3 full.

Bake 20–25 minutes or until an inserted toothpick comes out clean. Cool for 10 minutes before removing from pans.

✎ **Grocery list:** applesauce, carrots, Granny Smith apple, crushed pineapple, raisins, walnuts

✎ **Pantry checklist:** flour, sugar, cinnamon, nutmeg, baking soda, salt, eggs, vegetable oil, vanilla

OVERNIGHT OATMEAL-RAISIN MUFFINS

Yield: 2 dozen muffins

1 cup regular oats
♡*2 cups buttermilk*
1 2/3 cups whole-wheat flour
1 cup dark brown sugar
1/4 cup vegetable oil
1 teaspoon baking powder
1 teaspoon baking soda
1 teaspoon salt
2 large eggs, lightly beaten
1 cup golden raisins
1 cup chopped pecans

Combine oats and buttermilk in a medium bowl; cover and refrigerate overnight.

Preheat oven to 350 degrees.

Mix oat-buttermilk mixture with next 7 ingredients and mix well. Fold in raisins and pecans. Bake 15–17 minutes until done. Cool in pans 10 minutes before removing.

✎ **Grocery list:** oats, buttermilk, whole-wheat flour, golden raisins, pecans

✎ **Pantry checklist:** brown sugar, vegetable oil, baking powder, baking soda, salt, eggs

HEALTHY BANANA BREAD

Yield: 3 small loaves

3 large ripe bananas, mashed
3/4 cup vegetable oil
3/4 cup oats
3/4 cup sugar
3/4 cup whole-wheat flour
1/2 cup white flour
2 teaspoons baking powder
1 large egg
1 cup raisins
1 cup chopped walnuts

Preheat oven to 350 degrees.

Mix all ingredients together in a bowl. Place in 3 well-greased mini loaf pans. Bake 35 minutes or until done. Cool in pans 10 minutes before removing.

✎ **Grocery list:** bananas, oats, whole-wheat flour, raisins, walnuts

✎ **Pantry checklist:** vegetable oil, sugar, white flour, baking powder, egg

Zucchini Bread

Yield: 2 loaves

3 cups flour
1 teaspoon baking soda
3/4 teaspoon salt
1/2 teaspoon cinnamon
1/4 teaspoon cloves
1/8 teaspoon ginger
1/8 teaspoon nutmeg
1 cup chopped pecans or walnuts
3/4 cup chopped dates
2 cups shredded zucchini
1 cup granulated sugar
1/2 cup brown sugar
1 cup vegetable oil
♡1/3 cup milk
4 ounces applesauce
2 teaspoons vanilla
3 large eggs, lightly beaten

Preheat oven to 350 degrees.

Combine first 9 ingredients in a large bowl. Press zucchini between paper towels to remove excess moisture. In a separate bowl, combine zucchini with remaining ingredients and mix well. Add zucchini mixture to flour mixture, stirring just until dry ingredients are moistened. Pour batter into 2 greased loaf pans. Bake 30–35 minutes or until inserted toothpick comes out clean. Cool in pans 10 minutes before removing.

✎ **Grocery list:** pecans or walnuts, dates, zucchini, applesauce

✎ **Pantry checklist:** flour, baking soda, salt, cinnamon, cloves, ginger, nutmeg, granulated sugar, brown sugar, vegetable oil, milk, vanilla, eggs

Hospitality Note: This bread can be baked in advance and frozen.

Pumpkin Bread

Yield: 3 loaves

1 cup raisins
2/3 cup boiling water
3 cups sugar
1 cup vegetable oil
4 eggs, beaten
1 (1-pound) can pumpkin
1 cup chopped pecans

Dry ingredients:
3 1/2 cups flour
1 teaspoon baking powder
1/2 teaspoon baking soda
1 teaspoon salt
1/2 teaspoon cloves
1 teaspoon cinnamon
1 teaspoon nutmeg
1 teaspoon allspice

Preheat oven to 350 degrees.

Soak raisins in the boiling water for 5 minutes.

Meanwhile, combine sugar, oil, and eggs. Add pumpkin. Sift together dry ingredients and add to pumpkin mixture. Add pecans and raisins with water.

Pour into 3 greased medium-sized loaf pans. Bake 45–60 minutes or until done. Cool in pans 10 minutes before removing.

✎ **Grocery list:** raisins, pumpkin, pecans

✎ **Pantry checklist:** sugar, vegetable oil, eggs, flour, baking powder, baking soda, salt, cloves, cinnamon, nutmeg, allspice

Strawberry Bread

Yield: 2 loaves

3 cups flour
1 teaspoon baking soda
1/2 teaspoon salt
1 tablespoon cinnamon
2 cups sugar
3 eggs, beaten
1 cup vegetable oil
2 (10-ounce) packages frozen sliced strawberries, thawed and drained

Preheat oven to 350 degrees.

Combine first 5 ingredients and mix well. In a separate large bowl, mix eggs, oil, and strawberries. Add dry ingredients, mixing well. Pour batter into 2 well-greased loaf pans. Bake 1 hour or until inserted toothpick comes out clean. Cool in pans 10 minutes before removing.

✎ **Grocery list:** frozen sliced strawberries
✎ **Pantry checklist:** flour, baking soda, salt, cinnamon, sugar, eggs, vegetable oil

Loaf Bread

Yield: 3 loaves

2 packages dry yeast
2 1/2 cups warm water, divided
1/2 cup sugar
1/2 cup vegetable oil
1 tablespoon salt
5–6 cups flour

Mix yeast with 1/2 cup warm water and let set for 5 minutes or until it bubbles. Combine yeast with sugar, oil, salt, and remaining water in mixer using dough hook. Add flour, 1 cup at a time, until dough is the right consistency—a soft dough. Cover mixer and let dough rise until doubled. Turn mixer on to punch dough down. Cover and let rise again. Remove dough from mixer. Divide dough into 3 portions. Place each portion in a well-greased loaf pan and let rise until doubled in size. Preheat oven to 350 degrees. Bake 20 minutes. Remove from oven and cool on wire rack for 10 minutes before taking the bread out of the pans.

Grocery list: dry yeast
Pantry checklist: sugar, vegetable oil, salt, flour

WHOLE-GRAIN BREAD

Yield: 3 loaves

2 packages dry yeast
2 1/2 cups warm water, divided
1/4 cup sugar
1/2 cup vegetable oil
1 tablespoon salt
1/2 cup crushed oats
1/2 cup crushed wheat
1/2 cup pure bran
1 1/2 cups whole-wheat flour
2–3 cups white flour

Mix yeast with 1/2 cup warm water and let set for 5 minutes or until it bubbles. Combine yeast with sugar, oil, salt, and remaining water in mixer using dough hook. Add oats, crushed wheat, pure bran, wheat flour, and white flour, 1 cup at a time, until dough is the right consistency. Cover mixer and let dough rise until doubled. Turn mixer on to punch dough down. Cover and let rise again. Remove dough from mixer. Preheat oven to 350 degrees. Divide into 3 portions and place each in a well-greased loaf pan. Let rise again until doubled. Bake 20–25 minutes or until done. Cool on wire rack for 10 minutes before removing the loaves.

✎ **Grocery list:** dry yeast, crushed oats, crushed wheat, pure bran, whole-wheat flour

✎ **Pantry checklist:** sugar, vegetable oil, salt, white flour

Cloverleaf Rolls

Yield: 1 dozen rolls

1 package dry yeast
1¼ cups warm water, divided
¼ cup sugar
¼ cup vegetable oil
1½ teaspoons salt
2½ cups flour

Mix yeast with ¼ cup warm water and let set for 5 minutes or until it bubbles. Combine yeast with sugar, oil, salt, and remaining water in mixer using dough hook. Add flour, 1 cup at a time, until dough is the right consistency. Cover mixer and let dough rise until doubled. Turn mixer on to punch dough down. Cover and let rise again until doubled. Remove dough from mixer.

Punch dough down. Form into cloverleaf rolls and place in greased muffin tins. Let rise again until double. Preheat oven to 350 degrees. Bake 10 minutes or until browned. Cool in pans 10 minutes before removing.

✎ **Grocery list:** dry yeast
✎ **Pantry checklist:** sugar, vegetable oil, salt, flour

Note: You can use quick-rise yeast and eliminate the ¼ cup warm water.

MINIATURE LUNCHEON ROLLS

Yield: 20–25 cheese rolls, 20–25 walnut rolls

1 package dry yeast
1¼ cups warm water, divided
¼ cup sugar
¼ cup vegetable oil
2 teaspoons salt
2½ cups flour (more if needed)
♡20–25 cheddar cheese cubes
20–25 walnut halves, toasted

Mix yeast with ¼ cup warm water and let set for 5 minutes or until it bubbles. In a large mixer bowl, combine 1 cup warm water, sugar, oil, and salt. Add yeast mixture. Gradually add flour. Cover mixer and let dough rise until doubled. Punch down and let rise again. Remove dough from mixer. Divide dough in half. Make small balls from dough and wrap half of them around a cheese cube, half around a walnut half. Place rolls in greased miniature muffin pans and let rise until doubled. Preheat oven to 350 degrees. Bake 8–10 minutes or until lightly browned. Cool in pans 10 minutes before removing.

✎ **Grocery list:** dry yeast, cheese cubes, walnuts

✎ **Pantry checklist:** sugar, vegetable oil, salt, flour

> ***Hospitality Note:*** Fold a small, white lace doily in half and tuck one of each kind of roll inside for a ladies' luncheon plate.

Apricot Sweet Rolls

Yield: 18 rolls

1 package dry yeast
1¼ cups warm water, divided
¼ cup sugar
¼ cup vegetable oil
1½ teaspoons salt
2½ cups flour (more if needed)
1 (18-ounce) jar apricot preserves (reserve ¼ cup)

Mix yeast with ¼ cup warm water and let set for 5 minutes or until it bubbles. Combine yeast with sugar, oil, salt, and remaining water in mixer using dough hook. Add flour, 1 cup at a time, until dough is the right consistency. Cover mixer and let dough rise until doubled. Turn mixer on to punch dough down. Cover and let rise again. Remove dough from mixer.

Roll out dough on a lightly floured area; spread with apricot preserves. Roll up in jelly-roll fashion and cut into ¾-inch slices. Place in greased round cake pans and let rise until double. Preheat oven to 350 degrees. Bake 15 minutes or until lightly browned. Cool in pans 10 minutes before removing.

Note: You can use quick-rise yeast and eliminate the ¼ cup warm water.

Icing

¼ cup apricot preserves
2 tablespoons butter, melted
1 tablespoon water
1½ cups powdered sugar

Mix apricot preserves with melted butter, water, and powdered sugar. Drizzle over rolls.

✎ **Grocery list:** dry yeast, apricot preserves, powdered sugar
✎ **Pantry checklist:** sugar, vegetable oil, salt, flour, butter

Hospitality Note: These rolls make a wonderful gift when creatively packaged!

CINNAMON ROLLS

Yield: 18 rolls

My grandchildren's favorite

1 package dry yeast
1 1/4 cups warm water, divided
1/4 cup sugar
1/4 cup vegetable oil
1 1/2 teaspoons salt
2 1/2 cups flour (more if needed)
1/4 cup butter, melted
cinnamon

Mix yeast with 1/4 cup warm water and let set for 5 minutes or until it bubbles. Combine yeast with sugar, oil, salt, and remaining water in mixer using dough hook. Add flour, 1 cup at a time, until dough is the right consistency. Cover mixer and let dough rise until doubled. Turn mixer on to punch dough down. Cover and let rise again. Remove dough from mixer.

Roll dough out on a lightly floured area; spread with butter and sprinkle with cinnamon. Roll up in jelly-roll fashion and cut into 3/4-inch slices. Place in greased round cake pans and let rise until double. Preheat oven to 350 degrees. Bake 10 minutes or until lightly browned. Cool in pans 10 minutes before removing.

Icing

1 cup powdered sugar (or more)
2 tablespoons butter, melted
2 tablespoons water

Mix sugar, butter, and water. Drizzle over rolls.

✎ **Grocery list:** dry yeast, powdered sugar
✎ **Pantry checklist:** sugar, vegetable oil, salt, flour, butter, cinnamon

Sour Cream Cinnamon Rolls

Yield: 12–14 rolls

♡*1 (8-ounce) container sour cream*
2 tablespoons butter
1/4 cup granulated sugar
1/2 teaspoon salt
1/8 teaspoon baking soda
1 large egg, lightly beaten
1 package dry yeast
3 cups flour
2 tablespoons butter, softened
1/2 cup brown sugar
2 teaspoons cinnamon

Icing

1 1/2 cups powdered sugar
♡*2 tablespoons milk*

Heat sour cream in a small saucepan over low heat to 105–115 degrees. Spoon sour cream into mixer and add 2 tablespoons butter, sugar, salt, baking soda, egg, and yeast. Gradually stir in flour to make a soft dough. Turn dough out onto flat surface and knead 4–5 times. Let rest 5 minutes. Roll dough into large rectangle and spread with 2 tablespoons softened butter, then sprinkle with brown sugar and cinnamon. Roll dough in jelly-roll fashion; cut in 1-inch slices and place in greased muffin pans. Preheat oven to 350 degrees. Cover and let rise in warm place until doubled. Bake 12–15 minutes or until lightly browned. Remove from oven and cool 10 minutes.

Mix powdered sugar and milk for icing. Drizzle icing over warm rolls.

✎ **Grocery list:** sour cream, dry yeast, powdered sugar

✎ **Pantry checklist:** butter, granulated sugar, salt, baking soda, egg, flour, brown sugar, cinnamon, milk

CARAMEL SWEET ROLLS

Yield: 18 rolls

1 package dry yeast
1¼ cups warm water, divided
¼ cup vegetable oil
¼ cup sugar
1 teaspoon salt
2½ cups flour (more if needed)

Caramel Sauce
2 cups brown sugar
½ cup butter
♡*1 cup corn syrup*
1 cup chopped pecans

Mix yeast with ¼ cup warm water and let set for 5 minutes or until it bubbles. Combine yeast with oil, sugar, salt, and remaining water in mixer using a dough hook. Add flour, 1 cup at a time, until dough is the right consistency. Cover mixer and let dough rise until doubled. Turn mixer on to punch dough down. Cover and let rise again until doubled. Remove dough from mixer.

Mix caramel sauce ingredients together in a small saucepan and heat until well mixed. Then pour into 2 round cake pans. Shape dough into small balls and place on top of sauce. Cover with towel and let rise until doubled in size. Preheat oven to 350 degrees. Bake 15–17 minutes or until browned.

Let stand 2 minutes in pan and then turn upside down onto plate.

✎ **Grocery list:** dry yeast, pecans
✎ **Pantry checklist:** vegetable oil, sugar, salt, flour, brown sugar, butter, corn syrup

Focaccia

Yield: 8 servings

1 package dry yeast
1 teaspoon sugar
1 cup warm water
3 cups flour, divided
1/4 cup butter, softened
1/4 cup fresh rosemary leaves, chopped and divided
1/2 teaspoon salt
♡1/4 cup olive oil, divided
4 garlic cloves, minced
1 teaspoon kosher salt
1/4 teaspoon fresh ground pepper

Combine yeast, sugar, and water. Let stand 5 minutes.

Place 2 cups flour in a large bowl; make a well in center and add yeast mixture. Stir until a soft dough forms. Cover and let rise in warm place until doubled.

Sprinkle remaining 1 cup flour on flat surface; add dough and knead until flour is thoroughly mixed in to make a firm dough. Gradually knead in butter, 1/8 cup rosemary, and 1/2 teaspoon salt. Knead until dough is smooth and elastic (adding flour if necessary).

Brush cookie sheet with 2 tablespoons olive oil. Divide dough in half and flatten each portion to approximately 15 x 10 inches. Place on cookie sheet; cover and let rise for 30 minutes or until doubled in size.

Preheat oven to 375 degrees. Using fingertips, punch dough all over. Sprinkle with minced garlic and remaining rosemary. Drizzle with remaining olive oil; sprinkle with kosher salt and pepper. Bake 25–30 minutes or until golden brown.

✎ **Grocery list:** dry yeast, fresh rosemary

✎ **Pantry checklist:** sugar, flour, butter, salt, olive oil, garlic, kosher salt, pepper

BRUNCH

Be kindly affectionate to one another with brotherly love,
in honor giving preference to one another…given to hospitality.
—ROMANS 12:10–13, NKJV

One of the great things about brunch recipes is that there are so many dishes that can be partially or fully prepared in advance. This leaves more time for enjoying your guests!

I am blessed to be part of a special prayer group that meets every month. We eat together, pray together, and share what is going on in our lives. During the rest of the month, prayer requests for a special need are only a phone call away. These women are dear to me, and I cherish our times together. Recently I was hosting them for brunch and had prepared dishes the night before. Something urgent came up, and I couldn't host the next morning. So I called one of the women, Gwen, and asked if she would take my place as hostess. The table was set and the meal already prepared—the brunch just needed a last-minute heating. Gwen came and took care of getting the food out, and then the ladies cleaned it up. I'm not sure they even missed me! It pays to be prepared ahead of time.

Another reason brunch is one of my favorite meals to prepare is for the traditions it can begin. Long before I moved to Tennessee, for example, several of my friends and I came to Nashville every November to visit with one another and do our early holiday shopping. Paul and I have lived in Tennessee for eleven years now, and these friends are still coming. We begin our day with brunch and end it with chocolate. Each night before we go to bed, I place chocolates (purchased from thecocoatree.com) and small books about friends on their pillows. As they go upstairs, we all laugh and say as the Waltons used to say, "Good night, Mary Ellen. Good night, John Boy!" Good friends, good food, time well spent—what a gift!

TOMATO-PESTO TART

Yield: 7–8 servings

1 (15-ounce) package refrigerated piecrust
♡*1 tablespoon olive oil*
♡*1 cup shredded mozzarella cheese, divided*
♡*1 cup shredded cheddar cheese, divided*
5 plum tomatoes, sliced
1/4 cup freshly grated Parmesan cheese
♡*1/2 cup mayonnaise*
2 teaspoons Mrs. Dash
1 tablespoon dried or fresh basil
1/2 teaspoon pepper
3 tablespoons fresh basil

Preheat oven to 400 degrees.

Place piecrust in a large pie pan. Crimp edge and brush outer edge with olive oil. Bake for 8–10 minutes. After removing from oven, sprinkle with 1/2 cup mozzarella and 1/2 cup cheddar cheese and arrange tomato slices over cheese. Turn oven down to 375 degrees.

Stir together remaining mozzarella cheese and cheddar cheese, Parmesan cheese, mayonnaise, Mrs. Dash, 1 tablespoon dried or fresh basil, and pepper. Spread over tomatoes. Bake at 375 for 20 minutes. Sprinkle with fresh basil. Slice and serve.

✎ **Grocery list:** piecrust, mozzarella cheese, cheddar cheese, plum tomatoes, Parmesan cheese, fresh basil

✎ **Pantry checklist:** olive oil, mayonnaise, Mrs. Dash, dried basil, pepper

Quiche

Yield: 6 servings

1 piecrust
♡*3 slices bacon, cooked and crumbled*
♡*3/4 cup shredded Swiss cheese*
♡*3/4 cup shredded cheddar cheese*
1/2 package (10-ounce) frozen spinach
4 eggs, beaten
♡*1 cup milk*
♡*1 cup half-and-half*
1 tablespoon flour
1/4 teaspoon salt
1/4 teaspoon white pepper
1/2 teaspoon dry mustard
dash of nutmeg

Preheat oven to 400 degrees.

Roll piecrust to fit quiche dish and bake 4 minutes. Reduce heat to 350 degrees. Place bacon and cheeses on top of crust. Thaw spinach in the microwave on high for 3½ minutes. Drain well between paper towels. Mix spinach with remaining ingredients and pour over cheese. Bake 1 hour or until set.

✎ **Grocery list:** piecrust, bacon, Swiss cheese, cheddar cheese, frozen spinach, half-and-half

✎ **Pantry checklist:** eggs, milk, flour, salt, white pepper, dry mustard, nutmeg

SPINACH-TOMATO QUICHE

Yield: 6–8 servings

1 (10-ounce) package frozen chopped spinach, thawed
1 (14 1/2-ounce) can petite diced tomatoes, drained
1/2 cup seasoned croutons, crushed
3 large eggs, lightly beaten
♡1 cup half-and-half
♡1/2 cup shredded mozzarella cheese
♡1/2 cup shredded sharp cheddar cheese
1/2 teaspoon salt
1/4 teaspoon cayenne
1/2 teaspoon dried or fresh chopped basil
1 (9-inch) deep-dish frozen piecrust, unbaked
♡4 slices bacon, cooked and crumbled

Preheat oven to 350 degrees.

Drain spinach well; squeeze dry with paper towels in order to remove excess water. Set aside.

Mix tomatoes and crushed croutons in a small bowl and set aside. In a large bowl, combine spinach, eggs, half-and-half, cheeses, and seasonings. Then add tomato mixture. Pour into piecrust and top with bacon. Bake 40 minutes or until set. Let stand 20 minutes before cutting.

✎ **Grocery list:** frozen spinach, petite diced tomatoes, seasoned croutons, half-and-half, mozzarella cheese, sharp cheddar cheese, dried or fresh basil, piecrust, bacon

✎ **Pantry checklist:** eggs, salt, cayenne

Hospitality Note: Garnish with fresh rosemary stem.

Potato-Zucchini Quiche

Yield: 5–6 servings

Crust

1 egg, beaten
1/2 teaspoon salt
1 (1 pound, 4 ounces) package frozen shredded hash-brown potatoes, thawed
1/4 cup freshly grated Parmesan cheese

Preheat oven to 375 degrees.

In a large bowl, combine the egg, salt, hash browns, and Parmesan cheese. Mix well and press in bottom and up sides of a well-greased 9-inch pie plate. Bake 15 minutes or until crust is set and edges begin to brown. Reduce heat to 350 degrees.

Filling

1 large zucchini, thinly sliced
1 green onion, thinly sliced
♡*1 tablespoon olive oil*
1/2 cup finely chopped ham
1/4 teaspoon salt
1/4 teaspoon pepper
1/4 cup diced pimiento, drained
2 eggs
1 tablespoon Worcestershire sauce
♡*1/4 cup milk*
♡*3/4 cup Swiss cheese*

In skillet, sauté zucchini and onion in olive oil. Stir in ham, salt, pepper, and pimiento. Remove from heat and cool slightly. In a large bowl, beat eggs, Worcestershire sauce, and milk. Add zucchini-ham mixture and Swiss cheese. Pour over potato crust and bake 15–20 minutes or until set. Let cool for 5 minutes before cutting.

✎ **Grocery list:** frozen shredded hash-brown potatoes, Parmesan cheese, zucchini, green onions, ham, pimientos, Swiss cheese

✎ **Pantry checklist:** eggs, salt, olive oil, pepper, Worcestershire sauce, milk

BACON-TOMATO STRATA

Yield: 6 servings

1 green onion, sliced thin
♡*6 slices bacon, cooked and crumbled (save drippings)*
12 slices of very thin white bread
4–6 Roma tomatoes, sliced
♡*6 Swiss cheese slices*
4 large eggs
1 teaspoon salt
1/2 teaspoon pepper
1/4 teaspoon dried basil
♡*1 1/2 cups milk*
1/3 cup freshly grated Parmesan cheese

Cook green onion in 1 tablespoon bacon drippings in skillet until tender. Cut crusts from bread and arrange 6 slices in lightly greased 11-x-7-inch dish. Top with tomato slices, then layer with bacon, green onion, Swiss cheese, and 6 more bread slices. Whisk together eggs, salt, pepper, basil, and milk. Pour evenly over bread slices. Cover and refrigerate at least 4 hours. Preheat oven to 350 degrees. Bake 40 minutes or until set. Sprinkle with Parmesan cheese and bake 5 more minutes.

✎ **Grocery list:** green onions, bacon, very thin white bread, Roma tomatoes, Swiss cheese slices, Parmesan cheese

✎ **Pantry checklist:** eggs, salt, pepper, basil, milk

Sausage Breakfast Casserole

Yield: 8 servings

6–7 slices white bread (enough to fill 9-x-13-inch dish)
1 pound sausage, cooked and crumbled
♡3/4 cup shredded mozzarella cheese
♡3/4 cup shredded cheddar cheese
6 eggs, beaten
1 teaspoon salt
1 teaspoon dry mustard
♡2 cups milk
1 tablespoon Worcestershire sauce

Cut crusts from bread and place the slices in a greased 9-x-13-inch glass baking dish. Add sausage and sprinkle with mozzarella and cheddar cheese. Mix eggs with salt, dry mustard, milk, and Worcestershire sauce. Pour mixture over cheeses. Refrigerate overnight.

Preheat oven to 350 degrees. Remove from refrigerator 15 minutes prior to baking. Bake uncovered 45 minutes or until set.

✎ **Grocery list:** white bread, sausage, mozzarella cheese, cheddar cheese

✎ **Pantry checklist:** eggs, salt, dry mustard, milk, Worcestershire sauce

> ***Hospitality Note:*** Prepare this recipe with all ingredients except eggs, milk, and seasonings, and freeze in advance. Remove from freezer the night before serving, add remaining ingredients, and follow the directions for the rest of the recipe.

MEXICAN BRUNCH PIE

Yield: 6 servings

5 large eggs, beaten
2 tablespoons butter, melted
1/4 cup flour
1/2 teaspoon baking powder
♡*1 cup small-curd cottage cheese*
♡*2 cups shredded Monterey Jack cheese*
1 (4 1/2-ounce) can chopped green chilies, drained
1 tablespoon fresh cilantro

Preheat oven to 400 degrees.

Mix beaten eggs with butter, flour, and baking powder in a large mixer bowl at medium speed until mixture is well blended. Stir in cottage cheese, Monterey Jack cheese, chilies, and cilantro. Spoon into a well-greased pie dish.

Bake uncovered 10 minutes; reduce heat to 350 degrees and bake 20 more minutes or until set.

✎ **Grocery list:** small-curd cottage cheese, Monterey Jack cheese, green chilies, fresh cilantro

✎ **Pantry checklist:** eggs, butter, flour, baking powder

BREAKFAST PIZZA

Yield: 6 servings

♡*1 (8-ounce) package shredded Italian cheese blend, divided*
1 (16-ounce) Italian bread shell (thin)
3/4 cup fresh spinach leaves
3 Roma tomatoes, sliced
1 green onion, sliced
♡*6 slices bacon, cooked and crumbled, divided*
2 large eggs
♡*1/2 cup milk*
1/2 teaspoon pepper
1/2 teaspoon salt
1 teaspoon Worcestershire sauce

Preheat oven to 400 degrees.

Sprinkle half of cheese over shell; top with spinach, tomatoes, onion, and half of bacon. Whisk together eggs, milk, pepper, salt, and Worcestershire sauce. Pour into center of pizza and sprinkle with remaining cheese and bacon. Bake 20 minutes or until set.

✎ **Grocery list:** Italian cheese blend, Italian bread shell, fresh spinach, Roma tomatoes, green onions, bacon

✎ **Pantry checklist:** eggs, milk, pepper, salt, Worcestershire sauce

Easy Spinach Breakfast Pie

Yield: 6–7 servings

3 eggs

♡*1½ cups milk*

¾ cup biscuit mix

1 teaspoon salt

½ teaspoon cayenne

1 tablespoon Worcestershire sauce

1 (10-ounce) package frozen chopped spinach

♡*1 cup sharp cheddar cheese*

♡*½ cup mozzarella cheese*

Preheat oven to 350 degrees.

Mix eggs and milk together; blend in biscuit mix, salt, cayenne, and Worcestershire sauce. Thaw spinach in the microwave on high for 3½ minutes; then drain well. Stir spinach and cheeses into egg mixture. Spoon into greased 9-x-13-inch glass baking dish. Bake 35–40 minutes or until done.

✎ **Grocery list:** biscuit mix, frozen spinach, sharp cheddar cheese, mozzarella cheese

✎ **Pantry checklist:** eggs, milk, salt, cayenne, Worcestershire sauce

Hospitality Note: This recipe may be prepared, baked, and frozen ahead of time.

BACON CUPS

Yield: 10 servings

♡2 *(3-ounce) packages of cream cheese, room temperature*
♡2 *tablespoons milk*
1 *large egg*
♡1/2 *cup shredded Swiss cheese*
1 *green onion, chopped*
1 *tablespoon diced pimiento, drained*
salt or Mrs. Dash to taste
1 *package won ton wrappers*
♡5 *slices bacon, cooked and crumbled, divided*

Preheat oven to 350 degrees.

Beat cream cheese, milk, and egg at medium speed with an electric mixer until blended. Stir in Swiss cheese, green onion, pimiento, and salt or Mrs. Dash. Set aside.

Place won ton wrappers in muffin tins and bake 3–5 minutes or until lightly browned. Sprinkle evenly with half of the bacon and add the cream cheese mixture. Top with remaining bacon.

Bake 8–10 minutes or until set.

✎ **Grocery list:** cream cheese, Swiss cheese, green onions, pimientos, won ton wrappers, bacon

✎ **Pantry checklist:** milk, egg, salt or Mrs. Dash

Cranberry-Apple Casserole

Yield: 8 servings

3 cups chopped apples, peeled
2 cups fresh cranberries
2 tablespoons and 1/2 cup flour, divided
1 cup granulated sugar
3 packages instant cinnamon-spice oatmeal
3/4 cup chopped pecans
1/2 cup brown sugar
1/2 cup butter, melted

Preheat oven to 350 degrees.

Combine apples, cranberries, and 2 tablespoons flour, tossing to coat fruit. Add sugar and mix well. Place in a greased 2-quart casserole. Combine oatmeal, pecans, 1/2 cup flour, and brown sugar. Add butter, mix well, and spoon over fruit. Bake uncovered 45 minutes.

✎ **Grocery list:** apples, cranberries, instant cinnamon-spice oatmeal, pecans

✎ **Pantry checklist:** flour, granulated sugar, brown sugar, butter

> *Hospitality Note:* This also makes a great dessert served warm with vanilla ice cream.

Miniature Sausage Muffins

Yield: 20 miniature muffins

1/2 pound sausage, cooked and drained
3/4 cup biscuit mix
1/4 teaspoon cayenne
1/2 teaspoon dry mustard
1 tablespoon Worcestershire sauce
♡1/2 cup milk
♡1/2 cup shredded cheddar cheese
1 green onion, finely chopped

Preheat oven to 375 degrees.

Combine all ingredients and stir just until moistened. Spoon into greased miniature muffin pans and bake 12–14 minutes.

✎ **Grocery list:** sausage, biscuit mix, cheddar cheese, green onions

✎ **Pantry checklist:** cayenne, dry mustard, Worcestershire sauce, milk

FRENCH TOAST WITH PECAN SAUCE

Yield: 8–10 servings

4 large eggs, beaten
♡*2 cups milk*
1/2 teaspoon salt
1 teaspoon vanilla
1/2 teaspoon cinnamon
1 loaf French bread, sliced thick

In a large bowl, blend eggs with milk, salt, vanilla, and cinnamon. Dip French bread slices in egg mixture and brown in greased skillet on both sides until well done. Serve with maple syrup or sauce below.

Sauce

2 cups brown sugar
1/2 cup butter
1 cup corn syrup
1 cup chopped pecans, toasted

Combine brown sugar, butter, and corn syrup in saucepan. Heat until butter is melted and mixture is blended. Add pecans and serve over French toast.

✎ **Grocery list:** French bread, pecans
✎ **Pantry checklist:** eggs, milk, salt, vanilla, cinnamon, brown sugar, butter, corn syrup

SALADS

His mercy extends to those who fear him,
from generation to generation.
—LUKE 1:50

I guess you could say salads are the "in" food right now. They are simple to prepare, they are healthy, and they offer so many ways to be creative! Salad luncheons are also special because of the potential for variety—meats, vegetables, and fruits.

When I think of salads, I can't help but think of several years ago when I was recovering from minor surgery. My friends had filled our refrigerator with delicious salads for Paul and me to enjoy during my recuperation. One morning during this time, the telephone rang, and it was Michael. He and Debbie were at Kennebunkport with George and Barbara Bush and President Bush. He said, "Mom, someone wants to talk to you." It was President Bush!

The president asked if I had seen Michael and him playing golf on the news, and I had. I asked him if Michael had played well, and he joked, "He needs a little work." We both laughed. It was just like talking to a dear friend.

A few days earlier Michael had called and told us about how he had been watching George H. W. Bush fish from the rocks. Michael was a little concerned for him, although the Secret Service agents were nearby at all

times. Michael stayed close behind in case the former president slipped and fell. Suddenly, as the president cast his line, it whipped back, and the fly caught Michael on the ear. It only nicked him, so we were all able to laugh about the incident.

As I talked to the president of the United States that day, I remembered the first time I met his parents in 1989. It was such a privilege to meet them, and they have always been so kind and gracious to our family. They have passed along values in their own family, just as we have done in ours.

BLUEGRASS SALAD

Yield: 6 servings

2 heads romaine lettuce, torn
1 cup broccoli florets
1/2 cup blue cheese
1/2 cup dried cranberries
3/4 cup walnuts, toasted

Mix salad ingredients and serve with dressing below.

Dressing

♡*1/2 cup olive oil*
1/4 cup rice vinegar
1 tablespoon balsamic vinegar
3 tablespoons sugar

Whisk dressing ingredients together well and mix with salad ingredients just prior to serving.

✎ **Grocery list:** romaine lettuce, broccoli, blue cheese, dried cranberries, walnuts, rice vinegar, balsamic vinegar
✎ **Pantry checklist:** olive oil, sugar

QUICK TOSSED SALAD

Yield: 6 servings

1 head lettuce, torn
3 green onions, sliced thin
2 hard-boiled eggs, well done, peeled, and chopped
1 cup croutons

Dressing

♡*1 cup mayonnaise*
1 cup freshly grated Parmesan cheese
♡*1/2 cup Italian dressing*

Combine lettuce, green onions, and eggs in a medium bowl. Mix dressing ingredients and pour over salad. Add croutons.

✎ **Grocery list:** lettuce, green onions, croutons, Parmesan cheese, Italian dressing
✎ **Pantry checklist:** eggs, mayonnaise

Baby Blue Salad

Yield: 6 servings

1 bag mixed salad greens
4 ounces blue cheese, crumbled
1 (10.4-ounce) can mandarin oranges, drained
1 pint strawberries, quartered

Place salad greens on 6 salad plates; sprinkle with blue cheese. Distribute oranges and strawberries evenly on top. Top with dressing and the pecans of your choice (below).

Sugared Pecans

2 egg whites, room temperature
1 cup sugar
4 cups pecan halves
1/2 cup butter

Preheat oven to 325 degrees.

Beat egg whites until foamy. Gradually add sugar, 1 tablespoon at a time, and beat until stiff peaks form. Fold in pecans. Melt butter on large cookie sheet. Spread pecans over butter. Bake 30 minutes, stirring every 10 minutes. Cool and store in covered container.

Buttered Pecans

1/2 cup butter
4 cups pecan halves
1/2 teaspoon salt

Preheat oven to 300 degrees.

Melt butter on large cookie sheet. Add pecans and stir until well coated. Sprinkle with salt. Bake for 30–40 minutes, stirring every 10 minutes or until toasted. Drain on paper towels.

Dressing

1/2 cup balsamic vinegar
2 tablespoons Dijon mustard
3 tablespoons honey
2 garlic cloves, minced
1 green onion, minced
1/4 teaspoon salt
1/4 teaspoon pepper
♡*1 cup olive oil*

Whisk together dressing ingredients until well blended. Serve over salad.

✎ **Grocery list:** salad greens, blue cheese, mandarin oranges, strawberries, pecans, balsamic vinegar, green onions

✎ **Pantry checklist:** eggs, sugar, butter, salt, Dijon mustard, honey, garlic, pepper, olive oil

BROCCOLI WALDORF SALAD

Yield: 10 servings

6 cups broccoli florets
1 large red apple, chopped
1/2 cup raisins
1/4 cup chopped pecans
1/2 cup prepared coleslaw dressing

Combine the first 4 ingredients in a large bowl. Drizzle with dressing; toss to coat.

✎ **Grocery list:** broccoli, apple, raisins, pecans, coleslaw dressing

SALAD GREENS WITH MIXED FRUIT

Yield: 6 servings

8 cups mixed salad greens
1 1/2 cups fresh blackberries
1 1/2 cups fresh strawberries
2 kiwis, sliced
1 cup walnuts, toasted

Layer salad greens with blackberries, strawberries, kiwis, and walnuts. Serve immediately with blackberry dressing.

Dressing

1/2 cup seedless blackberry preserves
1/4 cup red wine vinegar
1 garlic clove, minced
1/2 teaspoon salt
1/2 teaspoon pepper
♡3/4 cup olive oil

Place dressing ingredients in blender. Mix thoroughly until smooth.

✎ **Grocery list:** mixed salad greens, fresh blackberries and strawberries, kiwis, walnuts, blackberry preserves

✎ **Pantry checklist:** red wine vinegar, garlic, salt, pepper, olive oil

Carrot-Apple Salad

Yield: 4–6 servings

2 Granny Smith apples, unpeeled and chopped
1 Red Delicious apple, unpeeled and chopped
1 cup shredded carrots
1 cup dried cranberries
2 tablespoons fresh lemon juice
1/2 cup sugar
♡*1/4 cup sour cream*
♡*1/2 cup mayonnaise (or more for better consistency)*
1/2 cup chopped walnuts

Combine apples, carrots, cranberries, and lemon juice in a medium bowl. In a separate bowl, mix sugar, sour cream, and mayonnaise. Blend well and stir in apple mixture. Top with walnuts and chill thoroughly.

✎ **Grocery list:** Granny Smith apples, Red Delicious apple, carrots, dried cranberries, lemon, sour cream, walnuts
✎ **Pantry checklist:** sugar, mayonnaise

Romaine-Orange Salad

Yield: 6 servings

1 package romaine lettuce
1 (8-ounce) can mandarin oranges
1/2 purple onion, sliced
1/2 cup pecans, toasted

Place ingredients in a bowl. Mix with dressing below just prior to serving.

Dressing

1/2 cup sugar
2/3 cup light olive oil
1 teaspoon dry mustard
1/4 cup apple cider vinegar

Mix ingredients in blender.

✎ **Grocery list:** romaine lettuce, mandarin oranges, purple onion, pecans
✎ **Pantry checklist:** sugar, light olive oil, dry mustard, apple cider vinegar

BROCCOLI SLAW WITH CRANBERRIES

Yield: 8 servings

1 package broccoli slaw
2 Granny Smith apples, chopped
1 cup dried cranberries
1/4 cup chopped purple onion
1/2 cup chopped walnuts, toasted

Mix together and serve with dressing below.

Dressing

1 cup vegetable oil
3/4 cup sugar
1/2 cup raspberry vinegar
1/2 teaspoon salt
1 clove garlic, minced
1/4 teaspoon ground white pepper

Combine dressing ingredients in jar. Cover tightly and shake vigorously. Pour over broccoli salad and marinate in the refrigerator 1 hour. Stir well before serving.

✎ **Grocery list:** broccoli slaw, Granny Smith apples, dried cranberries, purple onion, walnuts, raspberry vinegar

✎ **Pantry checklist:** vegetable oil, sugar, salt, garlic, white pepper

Strawberry and Mixed Greens Salad

Yield: 8 servings

1 pound spring greens mix
1 pint strawberries, sliced
♡*1 cup finely shredded Monterey Jack cheese*
1/2 cup chopped walnuts, toasted

Layer spring greens mix, strawberries, cheese, and walnuts in a large bowl. Top with dressing just before serving.

Strawberry Dressing

3/4 cup vegetable oil
1/3 cup sugar
1/4 cup red wine vinegar
1/8 teaspoon salt
1/8 teaspoon white pepper
1/4 cup strawberry jam
1 teaspoon poppy seeds

Combine dressing ingredients in a small bowl; whisk together until well mixed. Pour in jar and store in refrigerator until ready to use. To serve, shake dressing vigorously and pour over salad. Toss gently.

✎ **Grocery list:** spring greens mix, strawberries, Monterey Jack cheese, walnuts, strawberry jam, poppy seeds

✎ **Pantry checklist:** vegetable oil, sugar, red wine vinegar, salt, white pepper

Hospitality Note: Double this dressing recipe and keep in refrigerator for other salads.

SPRING GREENS AND FRUIT SALAD

Yield: 8 servings

1 pound spring greens mix
1 pint strawberries, sliced
1 pint blueberries
1 (10.4-ounce) can mandarin oranges, drained
♡*1 cup finely shredded Monterey Jack cheese*
1/2 cup chopped walnuts or pecans, toasted

Layer spring greens mix, strawberries, blueberries, oranges, cheese, and walnuts or pecans in a large bowl. Top with dressing just before serving.

Dressing

1 cup vegetable oil
3/4 cup sugar
1/2 cup red wine vinegar
2 cloves garlic, minced
1/2 teaspoon salt
1/4 teaspoon white pepper
1/2 teaspoon paprika

Combine dressing ingredients in a small bowl; whisk together until well mixed. Pour into jar and store in refrigerator until ready to use. To serve, shake dressing vigorously and pour over salad. Toss gently.

✎ **Grocery list:** spring greens mix, strawberries, blueberries, mandarin oranges, Monterey Jack cheese, walnuts or pecans

✎ **Pantry checklist:** vegetable oil, sugar, red wine vinegar, garlic, salt, white pepper, paprika

Hospitality Note: This is a great dressing to keep in refrigerator for other salads.

Orange and Poppy Seed Salad

Yield: 6 servings

Almond Topping

1 egg white
1/4 cup sugar
1 cup sliced almonds
2 tablespoons butter or margarine

Preheat oven to 325 degrees.

Beat egg white at high speed with electric mixer until foamy. Add sugar, 1 tablespoon at a time, beating 2–4 minutes until stiff peaks form and sugar dissolves. Fold in almonds.

Melt butter in baking pan in oven. Add almonds to pan, and bake 20–25 minutes (stirring every 5 minutes) until lightly browned. Cool.

Salad

1 head Bibb lettuce, torn
1 head green or red leaf lettuce, torn
1 (16-ounce) can mandarin oranges, drained
1 green onion, chopped

Toss together the lettuces, mandarin oranges, and green onion.

Dressing

♡3/4 cup olive oil
2/3 cup sugar
1/4 cup red wine vinegar
1 teaspoon grated orange rind
2 tablespoons fresh orange juice
1/2 teaspoon poppy seeds
1/8 teaspoon salt
1/8 teaspoon pepper

Mix dressing ingredients well. Drizzle over salad and toss. Sprinkle with sugared almonds and serve immediately.

✎ **Grocery list:** sliced almonds, Bibb lettuce, green or red leaf lettuce, mandarin oranges, green onions, orange, poppy seeds

✎ **Pantry checklist:** egg, sugar, butter or margarine, olive oil, red wine vinegar, salt, pepper

BROCCOLI AND ORANGE SALAD

Yield: 6 servings

♡3/4 *cup mayonnaise*
1/4 *cup sugar*
1 *tablespoon apple cider vinegar*
1 *head of fresh broccoli, broken into florets*
1/2 *small purple onion, chopped*
1/2 *cup golden raisins*
♡4 *slices bacon, cooked and crumbled*
1 *(11-ounce) can mandarin oranges, drained*
1/2 *cup sliced almonds, toasted*

Blend together mayonnaise, sugar, and vinegar in a large bowl. Add broccoli, onion, and raisins and chill for several hours. Prior to serving, top with bacon, oranges, and almonds.

✎ **Grocery list:** broccoli, purple onion, golden raisins, bacon, mandarin oranges, sliced almonds

✎ **Pantry checklist:** mayonnaise, sugar, vinegar

APPLE-SPINACH SALAD

Yield: 6 servings

1 *(10-ounce) package fresh spinach, torn*
2 *Red Delicious apples, thinly sliced*
1/4 *cup raisins*
1/2 *cup cashews*

Layer spinach, apples, raisins, and cashews. Serve with dressing below.

Dressing

1/4 *cup apple cider vinegar*
1/4 *cup sugar*
1/4 *cup vegetable oil*
1/4 *teaspoon garlic salt*
1/4 *teaspoon celery salt*

Combine dressing ingredients in a jar and shake well. Serve over salad.

✎ **Grocery list:** fresh spinach, Red Delicious apples, raisins, cashews

✎ **Pantry checklist:** apple cider vinegar, sugar, vegetable oil, garlic salt, celery salt

Raspberry Salad

Yield: 6 servings

1 (6 1/2-ounce) package mixed baby salad greens
2 cups fresh raspberries
♡*1/2 cup shredded mozzarella cheese*
1/2 cup sliced almonds, toasted

Dressing

♡*1/2 cup olive oil*
1/4 cup raspberry vinegar
2 tablespoons honey
1/2 teaspoon pepper
1/4 teaspoon salt

Place salad greens in a large bowl. Whisk together olive oil, raspberry vinegar, honey, pepper, and salt, mixing well. Toss salad with dressing and top with raspberries, cheese, and almonds.

✎ **Grocery list:** mixed baby salad greens, fresh raspberries, mozzarella cheese, almonds, raspberry vinegar

✎ **Pantry checklist:** olive oil, honey, pepper, salt

Broccoli-Fruit Salad

Yield: 8 servings

4 cups fresh broccoli florets, cut into small pieces
♡*8 slices bacon, cooked crisp and crumbled*
1 cup seedless red grapes
1 cup raisins or dried cranberries
1/4 cup chopped purple onion
1 cup chopped pecans or walnuts, toasted

Dressing

4 tablespoons sugar
1 tablespoon apple cider vinegar
♡*1/2 cup mayonnaise*

Place washed and well-drained broccoli in a large bowl. Add bacon, grapes, raisins or cranberries, onion, and pecans or walnuts. Mix together the dressing ingredients and pour over broccoli mixture. Refrigerate for several hours. Stir well prior to serving.

✎ **Grocery list:** fresh broccoli, bacon, seedless red grapes, raisins or dried cranberries, purple onion, pecans or walnuts

✎ **Pantry checklist:** sugar, apple cider vinegar, mayonnaise

APPLE-CASHEW SALAD

Yield: 4 servings

1 head red leaf lettuce, washed and torn
1 Granny Smith apple, thinly sliced
♡*4 ounces Swiss cheese, grated*
4 ounces cashews

Mix ingredients together and serve with poppy seed dressing below.

Poppy Seed Dressing

1 teaspoon poppy seeds
1/2 teaspoon salt
1/2 teaspoon dry mustard
1 tablespoon lemon juice
1/2 cup sugar
1/3 cup apple cider vinegar
1 teaspoon minced onion
1 cup vegetable oil

Mix first 7 ingredients in blender. Slowly add oil and mix until well blended. Store in refrigerator and shake thoroughly before serving.

✎ **Grocery list:** red leaf lettuce, Granny Smith apple, Swiss cheese, cashews, poppy seeds

✎ **Pantry checklist:** salt, dry mustard, lemon juice, sugar, apple cider vinegar, onion, vegetable oil

SOUTHERN POTATO SALAD

Yield: 6 servings

5 medium potatoes, peeled, cooked, and chopped
2 hard-boiled eggs, chopped
♡*1/2 cup mayonnaise*
♡*1/2 cup sour cream*
1/2 cup chopped celery
2 tablespoons chopped onion
2 tablespoons sweet pickle relish
1 tablespoon mustard
1 teaspoon salt
2 teaspoons sugar
1/2 teaspoon pepper
2 tablespoons diced pimiento, drained

Mix all ingredients together and chill. Then serve.

✎ **Grocery list:** potatoes, sour cream, celery, sweet pickle relish, pimientos

✎ **Pantry checklist:** eggs, mayonnaise, onion, mustard, salt, sugar, pepper

Asparagus-Vermicelli Toss

Yield: 6 servings

1 pound fresh asparagus, trimmed
7 ounces uncooked vermicelli
1 cup grape tomato halves
2 tablespoons fresh basil
1 green onion, sliced
1/4 teaspoon salt
1/2 teaspoon pepper
♡2/3 cup Italian dressing
1 teaspoon sugar

Cut asparagus into 2-inch pieces. Cook pasta according to directions, adding asparagus for the last few minutes of cooking. Drain. Rinse with cold water and drain again. Transfer asparagus and pasta to a bowl and add remaining ingredients. Mix well. Chill if desired.

✎ **Grocery list:** asparagus, vermicelli, grape tomatoes, fresh basil, green onions, Italian dressing

✎ **Pantry checklist:** salt, pepper, sugar

Crunchy Romaine Toss

Yield: 6 servings

1 cup chopped pecans, toasted
1 package ramen noodles, toasted and broken (discard flavor packet)
1 head romaine lettuce, washed and torn into pieces
1 (8-ounce) can mandarin oranges, drained
1 small purple onion, chopped

Mix ingredients and serve with dressing below.

Sweet-and-Sour Dressing

♡1/2 cup olive oil
1/2 cup sugar
1/4 cup red wine vinegar
1 1/2 teaspoons soy sauce
salt and pepper to taste

Blend dressing ingredients together and pour over salad just prior to serving.

✎ **Grocery list:** pecans, ramen noodles, romaine lettuce, mandarin oranges, purple onion

✎ **Pantry checklist:** olive oil, sugar, red wine vinegar, soy sauce, salt, pepper

GRAPE SALAD

Yield: 6 servings

♡1 *(8-ounce) package cream cheese, room temperature*
♡1 *(8-ounce) container sour cream*
½ *cup sugar*
1 *teaspoon vanilla*
6 *cups seedless red grapes, washed and dried*
1 *cup finely chopped pecans*

Mix first 4 ingredients well and then add grapes. (Important: grapes must be thoroughly dry or the filling won't stick.) Place in long casserole dish. Top with pecans. Place in refrigerator overnight. Delicious!

✎ **Grocery list:** cream cheese, sour cream, seedless red grapes, pecans
✎ **Pantry checklist:** sugar, vanilla

RAMEN NOODLE SALAD

Yield: 12 servings

1 *package ramen noodles, uncooked (discard flavor packet)*
1 *(16-ounce) package broccoli coleslaw*
2 *green onions, sliced*
4 *ounces almonds*
2 *tablespoons sugar*

Crumble noodles and mix with broccoli coleslaw and green onions.

Caramelize almonds in skillet by heating sugar and almonds over medium heat until the sugar is melted and almonds are turning brown. Top the salad with the almonds.

Dressing

¾ *cup vegetable oil*
⅓ *cup sugar*
2 *teaspoons red wine vinegar*

Mix dressing ingredients well and pour over salad.

✎ **Grocery list:** ramen noodles, broccoli coleslaw, green onions, almonds
✎ **Pantry checklist:** sugar, vegetable oil, red wine vinegar

Note: This salad is best if made the night or day before serving.

Cauliflower Salad

Yield: 12 servings

1/2 head lettuce, torn into small pieces
1 head cauliflower, cut into small pieces
1/2 purple onion, chopped
♡8 slices bacon, cooked and crumbled
1 cup dried cranberries
1 (8-ounce) can water chestnuts, chopped
1 cup freshly grated Parmesan cheese
♡1/2 cup mayonnaise
♡1/2 cup sour cream
1/4 cup sugar

In a large salad bowl, layer lettuce, cauliflower, onion, bacon, cranberries, water chestnuts, and Parmesan cheese. Mix mayonnaise and sour cream together and spread over salad. Sprinkle with sugar. Seal and refrigerate overnight. Toss well prior to serving.

✎ **Grocery list:** lettuce, cauliflower, purple onion, bacon, dried cranberries, water chestnuts, Parmesan cheese, sour cream

✎ **Pantry checklist:** mayonnaise, sugar

Cranberry-Pineapple Gelatin Mold

Yield: 6 servings

♡1 (3-ounce) package strawberry gelatin
♡1 (3-ounce) package orange gelatin
1 1/2 cups boiling water
1 cup finely chopped fresh cranberries
1 apple, peeled and chopped
1 stalk celery, chopped
1 (8 1/4-ounce) can crushed pineapple, undrained
1/4 cup chopped pecans (optional)

Mix strawberry and orange gelatins in boiling water until dissolved. Add cranberries and place in refrigerator until it begins to thicken. Then add remaining ingredients. Spoon into mold or square glass dish and chill until set.

✎ **Grocery list:** strawberry gelatin, orange gelatin, fresh cranberries, apple, celery, crushed pineapple, pecans

STRAWBERRY PRETZEL SALAD

Yield: 8 servings

2 tablespoons and 1 cup sugar, divided
2 cups crushed pretzels
1/2 cup butter, melted
♡1 (8-ounce) package cream cheese, room temperature
♡1 (8-ounce) container frozen whipped topping, thawed
2 cups boiling water
♡1 (6-ounce) package strawberry gelatin
1 (10-ounce) package frozen strawberries

Preheat oven to 375 degrees.

Mix 2 tablespoons sugar, pretzels, and butter and place in 9-x-13-inch baking dish. Bake 8 minutes, then cool in freezer.

Cream together 1 cup sugar and cream cheese. Add whipped topping and mix well.

Spread over cooled pretzel mixture; place in refrigerator until cream cheese mixture is firm. Mix boiling water with strawberry gelatin; stir until dissolved. Add frozen strawberries. Place gelatin mixture in refrigerator or freezer until it begins to thicken, then pour over cream cheese mixture, and chill until set.

✎ **Grocery list:** pretzels, cream cheese, whipped topping, strawberry gelatin, frozen strawberries

✎ **Pantry checklist:** sugar, butter

Lemon-Lime Creamy Salad

Yield: 8 servings

♡1 (3-ounce) package lemon gelatin
♡1 (3-ounce) package lime gelatin
1 cup boiling water
♡1 cup sour cream
♡1 cup mayonnaise
♡1 cup small-curd cottage cheese
3/4 cup finely chopped celery
1 (8 1/4-ounce) can crushed pineapple
1/4 cup diced pimiento, drained
1/2 cup chopped pecans
1 teaspoon prepared horseradish

Dissolve gelatins in boiling water. In another, large bowl combine remaining ingredients and mix well. Stir in hot gelatin, blending thoroughly. Pour into 9-x-13-inch glass baking dish and chill until set.

✎ **Grocery list:** lemon gelatin, lime gelatin, sour cream, cottage cheese, celery, crushed pineapple, pimiento, pecans, horseradish

✎ **Pantry checklist:** mayonnaise

Note: If you lightly spray dishes with a nonstick baking spray, gelatin salads will be easier to remove and serve.

> ***Hospitality Note:*** Garnish with maraschino cherries or fresh strawberries.

Frozen Cranberry Salad

Yield: 12 servings

1 (16-ounce) can whole cranberry sauce
♡1 (14-ounce) can sweetened condensed milk
♡1 (8-ounce) container frozen whipped topping, thawed
1 (8 1/4-ounce) can crushed pineapple, drained
1 cup chopped pecans, toasted

Combine all ingredients in a bowl and mix well. Spoon into 9-x-13-inch dish. Cover with foil and freeze.

✎ **Grocery list:** whole cranberry sauce, condensed milk, whipped topping, crushed pineapple, pecans

> ***Hospitality Note:*** For individual servings, freeze mixture in muffin tins.

FROZEN ORANGE AND PINEAPPLE SALAD

Yield: 18 servings

♡1 (8-ounce) package cream cheese, room temperature
1/2 cup sugar (or sweetener)
♡1 (8-ounce) container frozen whipped topping, thawed
1 (15 1/2-ounce) can pineapple tidbits, drained
1 (15-ounce) can mandarin oranges, drained
3 bananas, diced
♡2 tablespoons mayonnaise
2 tablespoons lemon juice
1/2 teaspoon salt
1 cup chopped pecans

Mix cream cheese and sugar until well blended. Add whipped topping and remaining ingredients. Freeze mixture in muffin tins.

✎ **Grocery list:** cream cheese, whipped topping, pineapple tidbits, mandarin oranges, bananas, pecans

✎ **Pantry checklist:** sugar, mayonnaise, lemon juice, salt

Hospitality Note: I keep this salad in the freezer at all times and use either as a salad or dessert.

Frozen Strawberry Salad

Yield: 12 servings

♡1 (8-ounce) *package cream cheese, room temperature*
1/2 *cup sugar*
♡1 (8-ounce) *container frozen whipped topping, thawed*
1 (8 1/4-ounce) *can crushed pineapple, drained*
1 (10-ounce) *package frozen strawberries, thawed*
2 *bananas, sliced*

Mix cream cheese and sugar in mixer until well blended; blend in whipped topping. Fold in pineapple, strawberries, and bananas and freeze in muffin cups.

✎ **Grocery list:** cream cheese, whipped topping, crushed pineapple, frozen strawberries, bananas
✎ **Pantry checklist:** sugar

Chicken Salad

Yield: 5 servings

5 *skinless, boneless chicken breasts, cooked and chopped*
♡3/4 *cup mayonnaise (or more)*
1/4 *cup sugar*
salt to taste
1 *tablespoon apple cider vinegar*
1 *cup chopped celery*
1/4 *cup diced pimiento, drained*

Combine chicken with remaining ingredients and mix well. You may need to vary the amount of mayonnaise depending on the size of the chicken.

✎ **Grocery list:** chicken breasts, celery, pimientos
✎ **Pantry checklist:** mayonnaise, sugar, salt, apple cider vinegar

Note: Add 1/2 cup dried cranberries and 1/2 cup toasted, chopped pecans for extra flavor. Adding grapes is another option.

SOUPS

Each one should use whatever gift he has received
to serve others, faithfully administering
God's grace in its various forms.
—1 PETER: 4:10

Soups are a favorite at our home. The weather doesn't have to be cold to enjoy them. They are simple to prepare and healthy, and when they are served with bread, crackers, salad, or fruit, they become a complete meal. They also are a comfort food that can be made in advance and shared with friends when an emergency arises.

Occasionally we invite twelve to fifteen young men who are friends for a night of food, fellowship, and fun at our house—"Guys' Night Out." I am the only female allowed, and that is because I prepare the food! What a great time we have together. They also think I ought to be doing this more often than I do. I really enjoy cooking for these young men, because they really enjoy eating!

Writing of "the guys" reminds me of when I was asked to teach a hospitality/cooking class at Belmont University. When I arrived, I was surprised to see several young men present. I had expected only women, so my first thought was, *This should be interesting.* My plan was to show them how to cook a turkey, pumpkin pie, and the Thanksgiving dinner fixings. As I began describing the preparations for the turkey, several of the young men and women began to say, "Do you mean I have to put my hand inside the turkey and pull that stuff out?" My anxiety about the class vanished, and we all began laughing. It turned out to be a great evening. I laughed and told them they could always fix a can of soup if the turkey was too complicated!

Relationships are what life is all about. We cannot have personal fulfillment without using the gifts God has given us to bless others. I pray that you will ask God for direction in your life as you share your gifts.

Cream of Asparagus Soup

Yield: 4 servings

4 tablespoons butter
4 tablespoons flour
1 teaspoon salt
♡*1 cup milk*
♡*1 cup chicken broth*
2 tablespoons white cooking sherry
1/8 teaspoon nutmeg
1 can (14.5-ounce) asparagus pieces
♡*sour cream and fresh parsley, to serve*

Melt butter in a medium saucepan. Add flour and salt, stirring while it thickens. Add milk, chicken broth, cooking sherry, and nutmeg. After it thickens again, add asparagus. Garnish with sour cream and fresh parsley.

✎ **Grocery list:** chicken broth, white cooking sherry, asparagus pieces, sour cream, fresh parsley

✎ **Pantry checklist:** butter, flour, salt, milk, nutmeg

Black Bean Soup

Yield: 5 servings

2 (15-ounce) cans black beans
1/2 cup salsa
1 tablespoon chili powder
1 (16-ounce) can chicken broth
♡*5 tablespoons sour cream*
5 tablespoons sliced green onions
2 1/2 tablespoons chopped fresh cilantro
♡*1/2 cup shredded cheddar cheese*

Place beans in a medium saucepan, partially mashing beans. Heat over medium heat, adding salsa, chili powder, and chicken broth. Serve in bowls topped with sour cream, onions, cilantro, and cheese.

✎ **Grocery list:** black beans, salsa, chicken broth, sour cream, green onions, cilantro, cheddar cheese

✎ **Pantry checklist:** chili powder

Tomato-Basil Bisque

Yield: 5 servings

♡2 (10 3/4-ounce) cans tomato soup
♡1 (12-ounce) can evaporated milk
1 (14 1/2-ounce) can petite diced tomatoes, drained
salt to taste
1/4 teaspoon pepper
2 tablespoons butter
2 tablespoons chopped fresh basil
fresh parsley, chopped, for garnish

Heat soup. Stir in milk. Add tomatoes, salt, pepper, butter, and fresh basil.

✎ **Grocery list:** tomato soup, evaporated milk, petite diced tomatoes, fresh basil, fresh parsley

✎ **Pantry checklist:** salt, pepper, butter

Hospitality Note: This soup is so delicious and easy to prepare.

French Onion Soup

Yield: 4 servings

3 cups thinly sliced onions
1 1/2 teaspoons sugar
1/4 teaspoon pepper
♡1/4 cup olive oil
♡2 (14-ounce) cans beef broth
4 slices French bread, toasted, or croutons
♡4 slices Swiss cheese

Cook onions, sugar, and pepper in olive oil for 20 minutes or until onions are caramelized, stirring frequently. Add broth and bring to a boil. Reduce heat and simmer for 30 minutes. Serve soup in bowls topped with French bread (or croutons) and cheese.

✎ **Grocery list:** beef broth, French bread or croutons, Swiss cheese

✎ **Pantry checklist:** onions, sugar, pepper, olive oil

Baked Potato Soup

Yield: 4 servings

5 tablespoons butter
5 tablespoons flour
♡3 cups milk
♡2/3 cup sour cream
1/4 cup finely chopped onion
2 baked potatoes, unpeeled and chopped
♡1 cup shredded cheddar cheese, divided
♡4 slices bacon, cooked and crumbled, divided
salt and pepper to taste
1 green onion, chopped

Melt butter in a large saucepan. Stir in flour until well mixed. Add milk slowly, stirring with whisk, and cook until mixture begins to thicken. Then add sour cream, onion, potatoes, half of cheese, salt, and pepper. Add half of the bacon. Cook 20 minutes. Serve in bowls topped with remaining bacon, remaining cheese, and green onions.

✎ **Grocery list:** sour cream, potatoes, cheddar cheese, bacon, green onions
✎ **Pantry checklist:** butter, flour, milk, onion, salt, pepper

Spinach-Mushroom Soup

Yield: 4 servings

2 tablespoons butter
1/2 cup fresh mushrooms
1 tablespoon finely chopped onion
2 tablespoons flour
♡2 cups milk
1 teaspoon salt
1/8 teaspoon pepper
1/4 teaspoon nutmeg
1 (10-ounce) package frozen chopped spinach, cooked in microwave and well drained

Melt butter in a medium saucepan and sauté mushrooms and onions for 3–5 minutes. Remove onions and mushrooms and add flour to pan and whisk until well mixed. Add milk, salt, pepper, mushroom mixture, and nutmeg and cook until mixture begins to thicken. Then add spinach.

✎ **Grocery list:** fresh mushrooms, frozen spinach
✎ **Pantry checklist:** butter, onion, flour, milk, salt, pepper, nutmeg

Fresh Spinach Soup

Yield: 4–5 servings

♡2 *(14-ounce) cans low-sodium chicken broth*
1/2 cup grated onion
1/2 cup grated carrot
1 teaspoon kosher salt
1/2 teaspoon fresh ground pepper
1/4 teaspoon nutmeg
6 tablespoons butter
6 tablespoons flour
♡*1 cup milk*
♡*2 cups cream*
6 cups fresh spinach, thinly cut in strips
fresh parsley, for garnish

Mix the first 6 ingredients together and simmer for 15 minutes.

Melt butter in another, large saucepan. Whisk in flour. Add milk and cream and blend well with whisk. Add chicken broth mixture and mix well. Add spinach and heat. Garnish with fresh parsley and serve.

✎ **Grocery list:** chicken broth, carrot, cream, fresh spinach, fresh parsley

✎ **Pantry checklist:** onion, kosher salt, pepper, nutmeg, butter, flour, milk

> *Hospitality Note:* Toasted sliced almonds also make a nice garnish for this soup.

Vegetable Soup

Yield: 6–8 servings

1 (32-ounce) can tomato vegetable juice
1/4 cup finely chopped onion
2 potatoes, diced
2 (10-ounce) packages frozen mixed vegetables
leftover roast (optional)
salt and pepper to taste
1 teaspoon sugar

Heat tomato juice in a large pot. Add onion and potatoes and cook until tender. Add frozen vegetables, roast (if desired), salt, pepper, and sugar. Simmer for 2 hours.

✎ **Grocery list:** tomato vegetable juice, potatoes, frozen mixed vegetables

✎ **Pantry checklist:** onion, roast (optional), salt, pepper, sugar

Simple Potato Soup

Yield: 4 servings

Paul's favorite

3 medium potatoes, peeled and chopped
1 stalk celery, chopped
1/4 cup finely chopped onion
1 cup water
♡2 cups milk
1/4 cup butter
salt and pepper to taste

In medium-sized pan cook potatoes, celery, and onion in water until tender. Add milk, butter, salt, and pepper. Cook until hot.

✎ **Grocery list:** potatoes, celery
✎ **Pantry checklist:** onion, milk, butter, salt, pepper

Ham and Potato Chowder

Yield: 4 servings

3 tablespoons butter
1/2 cup diced onion
1/2 cup diced celery
1/2 teaspoon dried thyme
2 cloves garlic, minced
1/8 teaspoon red pepper
3 tablespoons flour
♡1 (14-ounce) can chicken broth
♡1 cup milk
2 1/2 cups red potatoes, cubed and cooked
1 cup cubed ham
salt and pepper to taste
croutons, for garnish

Melt butter in a large saucepan over medium heat. Add onion, celery, thyme, garlic, and red pepper. Sauté until onion is cooked, stirring frequently.

Add flour and stir with whisk; cook 1 minute. Stir in broth and milk. Cook until mixture begins to thicken. Add potatoes, ham, salt, and pepper. Garnish with croutons.

✎ **Grocery list:** celery, chicken broth, red potatoes, cubed ham, croutons
✎ **Pantry checklist:** butter, onion, thyme, garlic, red pepper, flour, milk, salt, pepper

Chicken Pot Pie Soup

Yield: 4–6 servings

4 tablespoons butter
1/2 cup chopped onion
3/4 cup finely chopped celery
3/4 cup finely shredded carrot
1/4 cup chopped red pepper
1/4 cup flour
♡*2 (14-ounce) cans low-sodium chicken broth*
2 tablespoons cooking sherry
1/4 teaspoon white pepper
3/4 teaspoon kosher salt
1/8 teaspoon nutmeg
1 cup cooked and chopped chicken
1/2 cup corn, frozen or canned (drained)
1/2 cup peas, frozen
♡*1/2 cup half-and-half*

Melt butter in a large saucepan and add onion, celery, carrot, and red pepper. Cook for 5 minutes on medium-low heat until vegetables soften. Whisk in flour and cook 2–3 minutes. Stir in chicken broth, sherry, white pepper, kosher salt, and nutmeg. Add chicken, corn, peas, and half-and-half. Cook for 20–30 minutes. Remove from heat and serve.

✎ **Grocery list:** celery, carrot, red pepper, chicken broth, chicken, corn, peas, half-and-half

✎ **Pantry checklist:** butter, onion, flour, cooking sherry, white pepper, kosher salt, nutmeg

Entrées

Share with God's people who are in need.
Practice hospitality.
—Romans 12:13

My husband, Paul, and I have the privilege of working with the Room in the Inn program at our church. This program offers food, shelter, and spiritual nourishment to homeless men in our area. As Rev. Charles Stroebel, the director of the program, says, these men "find love, acceptance, and fellowship around the dinner table from those who so generously provide to help meet their needs."

Our core team serves these men by cooking, washing dishes, doing their laundry, operating a donated-clothes closet, and providing them with a shower, mattress, clean sheets, pajamas, toiletries, meals for the day, bus tickets, and all the spiritual encouragement they need.

Paul and I have received far more from this ministry than the men have received. We have met wonderful new friends who work with us. But words cannot describe the blessing we receive from the men themselves. For instance, one night after I had made bread and preserves for the program, one of the men asked if he could take a jar of preserves with him for the next morning. What a joy to give him that jar of preserves! It is in the giving that we are doubly blessed.

I'll never forget the night I met

Derek. He was a young guest, as so many of the men are. From the time he came in, we could tell he had a heavy heart. As we do most nights there, after dinner and a program that included a musical guest with a testimony, we asked for prayer requests and praises. Derek stood and asked us to pray for him. His young brother had recently died from AIDS, which he had known nothing about. He needed to tell his sick father about the death, and he still needed to bury his brother's ashes. He didn't know how he could handle this burden without God's help. He said he remembered his football days and wondered if we would surround him in a huddle to pray. By this time we were all sobbing.

Later that week we met Father Stroebel at the movie theater. He and a few other leaders were taking some of the men to see *The Passion of the Christ.* As we talked with them, we discovered that some of our volunteers had given money to provide transportation for Derek to visit his father and bury his brother. What a picture of true service—the main dish of life.

The dinner entrées we offer these men are just a part of the blessings that are given and received on those nights at Room in the Inn. As we gather around the table, we are to be a channel of God's love, joy, and peace to others.

Wild Rice Chicken Casserole

Yield: 8 servings

1 box long grain wild rice
2 tablespoons butter
2 stalks celery, finely chopped
1/2 onion, finely chopped
1 (8-ounce) can sliced water chestnuts, drained and chopped
2 cups cooked, chopped chicken (I usually use chicken tenderloins.)
♡*2 cups shredded cheddar cheese, divided*
♡*1 (10 3/4-ounce) can cream of chicken soup*
♡*1 cup sour cream*
♡*1/2 cup milk*
1/4 cup diced pimiento, drained
1/2 teaspoon salt
1/2 teaspoon pepper
1 cup soft breadcrumbs (homemade)
1/2 cup sliced almonds

Preheat oven to 350 degrees.

Prepare rice according to package directions.

Melt butter in a large skillet over medium heat. Add celery and onion and sauté 10 minutes or until tender. (You could also cook the celery and onion in the microwave.) In a large bowl, combine celery-onion mixture with water chestnuts, rice, chicken, 1 cup cheese, soup, sour cream, milk, pimiento, salt, and pepper and mix well. Spoon mixture into greased 9-x-13-inch glass baking dish and top with rest of cheese and breadcrumbs. Bake 30 minutes. Sprinkle with almonds; bake 5 more minutes.

✎ **Grocery list:** long grain wild rice, celery, water chestnuts, chicken, cheddar cheese, cream of chicken soup, sour cream, pimientos, almonds

✎ **Pantry checklist:** butter, onion, milk, salt, pepper, breadcrumbs

Lemon Grilled Chicken

Yield: 4 servings

4 (6-ounce) skinless, boneless chicken breast halves
5 teaspoons grated lemon rind
♡*1 tablespoon olive oil*
1½ teaspoons oregano
¾ teaspoon kosher salt
½ teaspoon black pepper
2 garlic cloves, minced
1 teaspoon Worcestershire sauce
4 lemon wedges
2 tablespoons chopped fresh parsley
rice, to serve

Spray outdoor grill with cooking spray and heat.

Place each chicken breast between 2 sheets of plastic wrap and flatten with rolling pin or meat mallet. Combine lemon rind and next 6 ingredients. Spread evenly on both sides of chicken and grill on both sides until done. Squeeze lemon wedge on each piece and sprinkle with parsley. Serve with rice.

✎ **Grocery list:** chicken breasts, lemons, fresh parsley

✎ **Pantry checklist:** olive oil, oregano, kosher salt, black pepper, garlic, Worcestershire sauce, rice

Chicken-Ranch Quesadillas

Yield: 4 quesadillas

2 cups chopped, cooked chicken breast
♡*½ cup ranch dressing*
½ cup salsa
1 package (8-inch) soft flour tortillas
♡*1 (8-ounce) package shredded mozzarella cheese*

Mix chicken, ranch dressing, and salsa together well. Spread chicken mix on a tortilla; top with cheese and add another tortilla. Grill in greased skillet until tortillas are browned and cheese is melted. This is delicious and so easy!

✎ **Grocery list:** chicken breasts, ranch dressing, salsa, tortillas, mozzarella cheese

HAWAIIAN CHICKEN

Yield: 6 servings

6 skinless, boneless chicken breasts
1 (20-ounce) can pineapple slices

Marinade

1 cup pineapple juice
1/3 cup soy sauce
2 tablespoons brown sugar
1 clove garlic, minced
1 teaspoon ginger
1/3 cup vegetable oil
fresh rosemary, for garnish

Spray grill with cooking spray and heat.

Mix marinade ingredients. Pour all but 1/2 cup of marinade over chicken, cover, and marinate several hours.

Cook on grill (or in a skillet) until done. Baste with 1/2 cup heated marinade and top with pineapple slices to serve. Garnish with fresh rosemary stems.

✎ **Grocery list:** chicken breasts, pineapple slices, pineapple juice, fresh rosemary

✎ **Pantry checklist:** soy sauce, brown sugar, garlic, ginger, vegetable oil

Note: I also grill pineapple slices for just a minute or so to lightly brown.

Hospitality Note: Keep this marinade in the refrigerator at all times; it can be used on pork, beef, and chicken.

Chicken-Almond Casserole

Yield: 4 servings

2 cups chopped, cooked chicken breast
1 cup chopped celery
1/2 cup and 1/4 cup slivered almonds, divided
2 hard-boiled eggs, chopped
♡*1/2 cup buttery cracker crumbs*
2 tablespoons minced onion
♡*1/2 cup mayonnaise*
1/2 teaspoon pepper
1 teaspoon lemon juice
♡*1 (10 3/4-ounce) can cream of chicken soup*
♡*1 cup crushed potato chips*

Preheat oven to 350 degrees.

Mix first 10 ingredients well and pour into greased 1 1/2-quart casserole. Top with 1/4 cup almonds and potato chips. Bake 30 minutes.

✎ **Grocery list:** chicken breasts, celery, almonds, cream of chicken soup, potato chips

✎ **Pantry checklist:** eggs, cracker crumbs, onion, mayonnaise, pepper, lemon juice

Easy Baked Chicken Breast

Yield: 4 servings

3 tablespoons vegetable oil
4 skinless, boneless chicken breasts
♡*2 (10 3/4-ounce) cans cream of chicken soup*
1 can water
salt and pepper to taste

Preheat oven to 350 degrees.

Heat oil in skillet. Lightly brown chicken and place in square baking dish.

Mix soup, water, salt, and pepper in skillet and heat. Pour gravy over chicken and bake 1 hour.

✎ **Grocery list:** chicken breasts, cream of chicken soup

✎ **Pantry checklist:** vegetable oil, salt, pepper

Hospitality Note: This chicken dish can be put together one day and baked the next.

MANDARIN CHICKEN

Yield: 4 servings

1½ pounds chicken tenders
¾ teaspoon salt
½ teaspoon black pepper
1 teaspoon butter
♡*2 teaspoons olive oil*
1 cup orange marmalade
2 teaspoons cornstarch
2 teaspoons lemon juice
1 teaspoon dry mustard
1 (11-ounce) can mandarin oranges
½ cup sliced almonds, toasted
rice, to serve

Sprinkle chicken with salt and pepper. Heat butter and oil in a large skillet. Add chicken and cook 4 minutes on each side until lightly browned. Remove from skillet and set aside.

Combine orange marmalade, cornstarch, lemon juice, and mustard in a small bowl, stirring mixture well with a whisk. Gently stir in oranges. Add mixture to skillet. Cover and cook 6 minutes on medium heat or until sauce slightly thickens. Spoon over chicken and sprinkle with almonds. Serve with rice.

✎ **Grocery list:** chicken tenders, orange marmalade, mandarin oranges, almonds

✎ **Pantry checklist:** salt, pepper, butter, olive oil, cornstarch, lemon juice, dry mustard, rice

Hot Chicken Salad

Yield: 6 servings

1½ cups chopped, cooked chicken
1 teaspoon grated onion
½ cup sliced water chestnuts
1 cup chopped celery
¼ cup diced pimiento, drained
♡¾ cup mayonnaise
½ teaspoon salt (or more for taste)
1 can bean sprouts, drained
1 teaspoon lemon juice
♡1 cup shredded cheddar cheese, divided
1 can rice noodles

Preheat oven to 350 degrees.

Mix chicken, onion, water chestnuts, celery, pimiento, mayonnaise, salt, bean sprouts, ½ cup cheese, and lemon juice together and spread in 9-x-13-inch greased baking dish. Top with remaining ½ cup cheese and bake 20 minutes or until hot. Remove from oven and sprinkle with rice noodles.

✎ **Grocery list:** chicken, water chestnuts, celery, pimientos, bean sprouts, cheddar cheese, rice noodles

✎ **Pantry checklist:** onion, mayonnaise, salt, lemon juice

Hospitality Note: This recipe can be put together a day in advance.

Creamed Chicken over Biscuits

Yield: 4 servings

2 large chicken breast halves
2 cups water
1 tablespoon chopped onion
1 stalk celery, sliced thin
3–4 tablespoons flour
salt and pepper to taste
2 tablespoons pimiento, drained
1 can refrigerated flaky biscuits, baked
buttered peas and cranberry sauce, to serve

Cook chicken breasts in water with onion and celery. When done, remove chicken from broth and chop. Add enough water to broth to make 2 cups and mix in flour, salt, and pepper. Cook until it begins to thicken. Add chicken and pimiento. Serve over baked biscuits with buttered peas and cranberry sauce.

✎ **Grocery list:** chicken breasts, celery, pimientos, refrigerated biscuits, peas, cranberry sauce
✎ **Pantry checklist:** onion, flour, salt, pepper

Chicken-Rice Noodle Casserole

Yield: 4–5 servings

2 cups chopped, cooked chicken breast
♡1 (10 3/4-ounce) can of cream of mushroom soup
1 can rice noodles, divided
1 cup chopped celery
1/2 cup sliced almonds
1/4 cup onion, chopped
2 tablespoons diced pimientos, drained
vegetable egg rolls and rice, to serve

Preheat oven to 350 degrees.

Combine chicken, soup, 1/2 can noodles, celery, almonds, onions, and pimiento. Mix well and place in 9-x-9-inch baking dish. Top with remaining noodles and bake 30 minutes. Serve with vegetable egg rolls and rice.

✎ **Grocery list:** chicken, cream of mushroom soup, rice noodles, celery, almonds, pimientos, vegetable egg rolls
✎ **Pantry checklist:** onion, rice

Chicken Parmesan with Spaghetti

Yield: 4 servings

4 skinless, boneless chicken breast halves
♡*1/2 cup buttermilk*
1 cup dry breadcrumbs
1/4 teaspoon salt
1/4 teaspoon pepper
♡*1/4 cup olive oil*
♡*4 slices mozzarella cheese*
8 ounces angel hair pasta, cooked and drained
1 (32-ounce) jar spaghetti sauce
1/4 cup freshly grated Parmesan cheese

Preheat oven to 350 degrees.

Dip chicken in buttermilk and then in breadcrumbs mixed with salt and pepper. Sauté the chicken in olive oil until browned on both sides. Place in lightly greased baking dish and bake 45–50 minutes. Remove from oven and top with mozzarella cheese; bake another 5 minutes until cheese is melted. Serve with pasta, covering pasta and chicken with sauce and Parmesan cheese.

✎ **Grocery list:** chicken breasts, buttermilk, mozzarella cheese, angel hair pasta, spaghetti sauce, Parmesan cheese

✎ **Pantry checklist:** dry breadcrumbs, salt, pepper, olive oil

Spicy Salsa Chicken

Yield: 4 servings

4 skinless, boneless chicken breasts
3/4 cup ketchup
1/2 cup salsa
1/4 cup honey
1 teaspoon Dijon mustard
1 teaspoon chili powder
1 teaspoon cumin
rice, to serve

Preheat oven to 350 degrees.

Place chicken in square or round glass baking dish. Blend remaining ingredients together and pour over chicken. Bake 45–55 minutes or until tender. Serve with rice.

✎ **Grocery list:** chicken breasts, salsa

✎ **Pantry checklist:** ketchup, honey, Dijon mustard, chili powder, cumin, rice

CHILI-SPINACH CHICKEN

Yield: 6 servings

1 (10-ounce) package frozen, chopped spinach, thawed and drained
♡2 tablespoons olive oil
1/4 cup chopped onion
2 green onions, chopped
1 (4 1/2-ounce) can chopped green chilies, drained
♡1 (10 3/4-ounce) can cream of chicken soup
1 (14 1/2-ounce) can petite diced tomatoes, drained
♡1 (8-ounce) container sour cream
1/2 teaspoon ground cumin
2 cups chopped, cooked chicken
♡1 (12-ounce) package tortilla chips
1 (8-ounce) package shredded Mexican 4-cheese blend, divided

Preheat oven to 350 degrees.

Press spinach between paper towels to make sure it is well drained.

In a large skillet heat olive oil, onion, green onions, and chilies and sauté until tender. Remove skillet from heat and stir in spinach, soup, tomatoes, sour cream, cumin, and chicken.

In a lightly greased 9-x-13-inch baking dish layer one half of tortilla chips, chicken-spinach mixture, and cheese. Repeat layers. Bake 20–25 minutes.

✎ **Grocery list:** frozen spinach, green onions, green chilies, cream of chicken soup, petite diced tomatoes, sour cream, chicken, tortilla chips, Mexican cheese

✎ **Pantry checklist:** olive oil, onion, cumin

Mexican Chicken

Yield: 6 servings

1 medium onion, chopped
1 green bell pepper, chopped
1 red bell pepper, chopped
♡2 tablespoons olive oil
♡1 (10¾-ounce) can cream of chicken soup
♡1 (10¾-ounce) can cream of mushroom soup
1 (10-ounce) can diced tomatoes with green chilies
1 teaspoon chili powder
1 teaspoon ground cumin
3 cups chopped, cooked chicken
♡2 cups crushed tortilla chips
♡2 cups (8 ounces) shredded cheddar cheese

Preheat oven to 350 degrees.

Sauté onion and peppers in oil until tender, about 5 minutes. In a large bowl, combine onion mixture, soups, tomatoes, chili powder, and cumin. Stir in chicken and mix well.

Place half of tortilla chips in lightly greased 9-x-13-inch glass baking dish. Add half of chicken mixture and half of cheese; repeat layers, ending with cheese.

Bake uncovered 30–40 minutes or until mixture is thoroughly heated.

✎ **Grocery list:** green pepper, red pepper, cream of chicken soup, cream of mushroom soup, diced tomatoes with green chilies, chicken, tortilla chips, cheddar cheese

✎ **Pantry checklist:** onion, olive oil, chili powder, cumin

Easy Turkey Breast

Yield: 6–8 servings (depending on size of turkey breast)

1 turkey breast
1 stalk celery, chopped

Place turkey breast in large, lightly greased pan. Add enough water to half cover turkey. Add celery. Cover and cook on stove top on medium to low heat for 2½–3 hours. When turkey is tender, turn over in broth and let it cool. Then refrigerate overnight. When ready to serve, remove turkey and slice. Also remove fat from broth and discard; use broth for gravy and dressing.

✎ **Grocery list:** turkey breast, celery

Note: This is a very moist turkey breast.

Kentucky Hot Brown

Yield: 4 servings

4 slices French bread, toasted (or any bread you prefer)
½ pound roasted turkey (from deli)
♡8 slices bacon, cooked crisp
1 large tomato, sliced thin

Cheese Sauce

¼ cup butter
4 tablespoons flour
♡1½ cups milk
♡1 cup cheddar cheese
¼ teaspoon salt
dash cayenne

Melt butter in saucepan; whisk in flour and cook until smooth. Add milk and cook until mixture thickens. Add cheese, salt, and cayenne.

Assemble each plate with toast, topped with turkey. Cover with cheese sauce. Then top with tomato slices and bacon.

✎ **Grocery list:** French bread, turkey, bacon, tomato, cheddar cheese

✎ **Pantry checklist:** butter, flour, milk, salt, cayenne

> *Hospitality Note:* Easy and delicious! Serve with steamed broccoli.

Tilapia with Vegetables and Basil Cream

Yield: 4 servings

4 tablespoons butter
1 medium onion, chopped
1 green pepper, chopped
1 red pepper, chopped
3 stalks celery, chopped
salt and pepper to taste
1/2 cup flour
1/4 cup cornmeal
4 (6- or 8-ounce) tilapia (fish) fillets
♡*1/2 cup buttermilk*
♡*4 tablespoons olive oil*
♡*1 cup cream or milk*
2 tablespoons chopped fresh basil
1/2 teaspoon salt
1/2 teaspoon pepper or Mrs. Dash
1 (15-ounce) can black beans, drained (optional)
1 (11-ounce) can sweet yellow corn, drained
1/4 cup cooking sherry

Melt butter in a large skillet. Add onion, green and red peppers, and celery and sauté 6–8 minutes or until tender. Stir in 1/2 teaspoon salt and 1/2 teaspoon pepper or Mrs. Dash. Spoon into serving dish and keep warm.

Combine flour and cornmeal. Dip fillets in buttermilk and dredge in flour mixture.

Heat olive oil in skillet and cook fillets over medium heat 3–4 minutes on each side until golden or fish flakes easily. Remove from skillet and keep warm.

Add cream or milk to skillet, stirring to loosen particles from bottom of skillet. Add chopped basil, sherry, salt and pepper to taste, and cook, stirring often until thickened.

Add beans and corn to celery-pepper mixture. Add fillets on top. Serve sauce over fillets.

✎ **Grocery list:** green pepper, red pepper, celery, tilapia, buttermilk, fresh basil, black beans, corn

✎ **Pantry checklist:** butter, onion, salt, pepper or Mrs. Dash, flour, cornmeal, olive oil, cream or milk, cooking sherry

CITRUS-BAKED FISH

Yield: 4 servings

1 pound orange roughy, tilapia, or fish of your choice
♡2–3 tablespoons olive oil
1/3 cup finely chopped onion
1 clove garlic, minced
2 tablespoons snipped fresh parsley
1 teaspoon finely shredded orange peel
1/2 teaspoon salt
1/4 teaspoon pepper
1/4 cup orange juice
2 tablespoons fresh lemon juice
lemon slices, to serve

Preheat oven to 375 degrees.

Place fish in a lightly greased baking dish. In a small saucepan mix olive oil, onion, and garlic. Cook until tender and remove from heat. Stir in parsley, orange peel, salt, pepper, orange juice, and lemon juice and pour over fish. Bake 15 minutes or until fish flakes easily with fork. When serving, spoon juices from dish over fish and top with fresh lemon slices.

✎ **Grocery list:** fish, parsley, orange, lemons
✎ **Pantry checklist:** olive oil, onion, garlic, salt, pepper

CRUSTED FISH

Yield: 4 servings

4 fish filets of your choice (orange roughy, tilapia, and cod work well)
1/2 cup coarse breadcrumbs
1/2 cup freshly grated Parmesan cheese
♡1/2 cup crushed plain potato chips
1/2 teaspoon paprika
1/4 teaspoon cayenne
2 tablespoons butter, melted

Preheat oven to 400 degrees.

Place fish in a greased baking dish. Mix breadcrumbs with Parmesan cheese, crushed potato chips, paprika, and cayenne. Toss with melted butter. Divide crumb mixture into fourths, pressing one portion on each piece of fish. Bake 15–20 minutes or until fish flakes.

✎ **Grocery list:** fish, Parmesan cheese, potato chips
✎ **Pantry checklist:** breadcrumbs, paprika, cayenne, butter

Baked Salmon with Salsa

Yield: 6 servings

2 pounds fresh salmon
♡2 tablespoons olive oil
1 tablespoon garlic salt
1 tablespoon garlic pepper
1 tablespoon paprika

Preheat oven to 350 degrees.

Place salmon in greased glass baking dish. Brush with olive oil and sprinkle with the 3 spices. Bake 15–18 minutes.

Salsa

♡1/4 cup olive oil
2 stalks celery, chopped
1/4 cup chopped onion
1/4 cup chopped red pepper
salt and pepper to taste
1 (15-ounce) can black beans, drained and rinsed
1 (15-ounce) can sweet yellow corn, drained
3 tablespoons chopped fresh cilantro

Heat olive oil in pan. Add celery, onion, red pepper, salt, and pepper. Cook until tender. Just before serving, add beans, corn, and cilantro and heat. Serve with salmon.

✎ **Grocery list:** salmon, celery, black beans, yellow corn, red pepper, cilantro
✎ **Pantry checklist:** olive oil, garlic salt, garlic pepper, paprika, onion, salt, pepper

Note: You can skip the salsa and serve with rémoulade or tartar sauce.

Rémoulade Sauce

♡1 cup mayonnaise
♡1/2 cup sour cream
2 tablespoons lemon juice
1 1/2 teaspoons Dijon mustard
1 tablespoon dried dill
1 tablespoon honey
salt and pepper to taste

Tartar Sauce

♡1 cup mayonnaise
2 tablespoons sweet pickle relish
1 tablespoon grated onion
1 teaspoon Dijon mustard
1 teaspoon honey
salt and pepper to taste

Mix all ingredients in each of the sauces to serve with fish.

✎ **Grocery list** (for sauces): sour cream

✎ **Pantry checklist** (for sauces): mayonnaise, lemon juice, Dijon mustard, dill, honey, salt, pepper, pickle relish, onion

Hospitality Note: I also add oven-roasted asparagus spears (see page 121) to the serving platter. Or you could prepare as directed and serve with sautéed spinach and mashed potatoes. Garnish with rosemary or parsley.

Bay Crab Cakes

Yield: 6 crab cakes

1 pound lump crabmeat
1 1/4 cups Italian breadcrumbs, divided
2 tablespoons flour
2 teaspoons fresh parsley
2 tablespoons chopped pimiento, drained
1 green onion, finely chopped
3 eggs, beaten
1 teaspoon dry mustard
1 tablespoon Worcestershire sauce
1/2 teaspoon cayenne
1/2 teaspoon kosher salt
1/4 teaspoon pepper
♡*olive oil*

Combine crabmeat with 1/4 cup breadcrumbs and remaining ingredients (except for olive oil) and mix well. Place in refrigerator for a couple of hours. When ready to cook, heat oil in frying pan. Shape crabmeat mixture into patties and dredge in 1 cup breadcrumbs. Cook over medium heat until browned, turning once. Drain on paper towels.

✎ **Grocery list:** crabmeat, Italian breadcrumbs, fresh parsley, pimientos, green onions

✎ **Pantry checklist:** flour, eggs, dry mustard, Worcestershire sauce, cayenne, kosher salt, pepper, olive oil

> ***Hospitality Note:*** This is great served with cocktail sauce (see page 16).

Easy Baked Pork Chops

Yield: 4 servings

vegetable oil
4 (1-inch-thick) pork chops
♡*2 (10 3/4-ounce) cans cream of chicken soup*
1 soup can water
3 tablespoons Kitchen Bouquet
salt and pepper to taste

Heat oil in skillet, brown pork chops, and place in greased glass baking dish. Add soup, water, Kitchen Bouquet, salt, and pepper to skillet. Mix well and heat. Pour gravy over pork chops and bake 1 1/2–2 hours.

✎ **Grocery list:** pork chops, cream of chicken soup

✎ **Pantry checklist:** vegetable oil, Kitchen Bouquet, salt, pepper

BRAISED PORK LOIN WITH PORT AND PRUNES

Yield: 8 servings

1½ teaspoons black pepper
1 teaspoon salt
1 teaspoon dry mustard
1 teaspoon dried sage
½ teaspoon dried thyme
1 (3–4 pound) boneless pork loin roast
♡*1 tablespoon olive oil*
2 cups sliced onion
1 cup finely chopped carrot
1 cup red cooking wine
♡*1 (14-ounce) can low-sodium chicken broth*
1 cup pitted prunes (about 20)
2 bay leaves

Preheat oven to 350 degrees.

To prepare spice rub, combine first 5 ingredients. Trim fat from pork; rub surface of roast with spice rub. Secure at 2-inch intervals with heavy string.

Heat oil in a large Dutch oven over medium-high heat. Add pork; cook 8 minutes, browning on all sides. Remove from pan. Add onion and carrot to pan. Cover, reduce heat, and cook 5 minutes, stirring frequently. Stir in wine and broth, scraping pan to loosen browned bits. Return pork to pan; add prunes and bay leaves. Bake 2 hours or until tender; discard bay leaves.

Place roast on a platter; cover with foil. Remove prunes with a slotted spoon. Place prunes in a food processor or blender; process until smooth. Stir puréed prunes into wine mixture in pan. Slice roast and cover with prune sauce.

✎ **Grocery list:** pork loin roast, carrots, chicken broth, prunes

✎ **Pantry checklist:** pepper, salt, dry mustard, sage, thyme, olive oil, onion, red cooking wine, bay leaves

Hospitality Note: Serve with mashed potatoes and a green vegetable. It may seem like a lot of preparation, but it is worth it!

Cranberry-Pineapple Pork Roast or Tenderloin

Roast Yield: 8 servings
Tenderloin Yield: 6 servings

♡*1 small bottle Catalina dressing*
½ cup pineapple preserves
1 package dry onion soup mix
1 can jellied cranberry sauce
1 large pork roast or tenderloin
wild rice and buttered broccoli, to serve

Preheat oven to 325 degrees for roast, 375 degrees for tenderloin.

Mix Catalina dressing, preserves, dry onion soup mix, and cranberry sauce together with a whisk. Place meat in large, well-greased baking dish and cover with the dressing mix. Bake roast for 2–3 hours or until well done. For tenderloin, cook 45 minutes. Cool 10 minutes before slicing.

Serve with wild rice and buttered broccoli.

✎ **Grocery list:** Catalina dressing, pineapple preserves, dry onion soup mix, jellied cranberry sauce, pork roast or tenderloin, wild rice, broccoli
✎ **Pantry checklist:** butter

Ham Loaf

Yield: 5–6 servings

2 pounds ground ham (I use a food processor.)
♡*½ cup milk*
¼ teaspoon pepper
1 cup soft breadcrumbs
2 eggs, beaten

Sauce

¼ cup vinegar
½ cup brown sugar
1 teaspoon Dijon mustard
¼ cup water

Preheat oven to 350 degrees.

Mix ground ham, milk, pepper, breadcrumbs, and eggs and place in greased loaf pan.

Mix sauce ingredients together and pour on top of ham loaf. Bake 1 hour.

✎ **Grocery list:** ham
✎ **Pantry checklist:** milk, pepper, breadcrumbs, eggs, vinegar, brown sugar, Dijon mustard

ASIAN PORK TENDERLOIN

Yield: 6 servings

1/3 cup light soy sauce
♡*1/4 cup olive oil*
1/3 cup brown sugar
2 tablespoons Worcestershire sauce
2 tablespoons lemon juice
1 tablespoon dry mustard
1 1/2 teaspoons pepper
4 garlic cloves, crushed
1 1/2–2 pound pork tenderloin

Preheat oven to 375 degrees.

Mix first 8 ingredients together. Place pork in a large baking dish and pour marinade over it. Cover and refrigerate overnight. When ready to cook, discard marinade and place pork in glass baking dish. Bake 30–40 minutes or until done. Let set for 5 minutes before slicing.

✎ **Grocery list:** pork tenderloin
✎ **Pantry checklist:** soy sauce, olive oil, brown sugar, Worcestershire sauce, lemon juice, dry mustard, pepper, garlic

Hospitality Note: Serve with Cranberry and Pecan Rice (see page 122).

Slow Cooker Roast

Yield: 8 servings

2 onions, sliced
2 teaspoons salt
1/2 teaspoon pepper
1 (3–4 pound) rump roast
1 tablespoon vegetable oil
1/4 cup water
2 tablespoons Worcestershire sauce
3 tablespoons flour

Place onions in bottom of 4-quart electric slow cooker. Combine salt and pepper and rub on roast. Heat oil in skillet and add roast. Brown roast on all sides and then place on top of onions in slow cooker. Cover and cook on high 1 hour. Reduce to low setting and cook 7 hours or until meat is tender. Remove roast and onion. Combine water, Worcestershire sauce, and flour and stir into drippings in cooker. Cook, uncovered, on high for 10 minutes or until thickened. Then pour over roast.

✎ **Grocery list:** rump roast
✎ **Pantry checklist:** onions, salt, pepper, vegetable oil, Worcestershire sauce, flour

Caramelized-Onion Pork Tenderloin

Yield: 6 servings

1 large sweet onion, thinly sliced
1 teaspoon sugar
♡*2 teaspoons olive oil*
1 pork tenderloin
salt, pepper, and garlic pepper to taste

Preheat oven to 375 degrees.

Cook onion and sugar in oil in skillet over medium to low heat until onion is tender and golden brown, about 20–30 minutes, stirring occasionally.

Place pork tenderloin in lightly greased baking dish. Sprinkle with salt, pepper, and garlic pepper.

Bake uncovered 30–40 minutes or until done. Let stand 5 minutes before slicing. Serve with onions.

✎ **Grocery list:** sweet onion, pork tenderloin
✎ **Pantry checklist:** sugar, olive oil, salt, pepper, garlic pepper

SIRLOIN TIP ROAST

Yield: 8 servings

3–5 pound sirloin tip roast
salt
garlic pepper
garlic salt
♡*2 (10 3/4-ounce) cans cream of mushroom soup*
3 tablespoons Kitchen Bouquet

Preheat oven to 350 degrees.

Prior to the day you want to serve, place roast in large, lightly greased roasting pan. Sprinkle with salt and garlic pepper. Add enough water to half cover the meat. Cover roast and bake 3 hours. Remove from oven, turn roast over in broth, cool, and place in refrigerator overnight.

The next day remove fat with slotted spoon and reserve broth. Slice roast on cutting board to desired thickness. Place slices in lightly greased glass baking dish and sprinkle with garlic salt between slices. Heat broth from roast in a medium saucepan. Add mushroom soup and Kitchen Bouquet and mix well. Heat and pour over roast.

✎ **Grocery list:** sirloin tip roast, cream of mushroom soup

✎ **Pantry checklist:** salt, garlic pepper, garlic salt, Kitchen Bouquet

EYE OF ROUND ROAST

Yield: 6 servings

1 eye of round roast
♡*1 (10 3/4-ounce) can cream of chicken soup*
1 package dry onion soup mix
salt and pepper to taste
2 tablespoons Kitchen Bouquet

Preheat oven to 350 degrees.

Place roast in foil large enough to seal well. Mix soup, onion soup mix, salt, pepper, and Kitchen Bouquet. Cover roast with soup mixture. Seal well and place in baking dish. Bake 2 1/2 hours.

Grocery list: round roast, cream of chicken soup, dry onion soup mix

Pantry checklist: salt and pepper, Kitchen Bouquet

> *Hospitality Note:* Delicious served with mashed potatoes and green beans.

Chili

Yield: 6–8 servings

♡1 pound ground chuck, cooked and crumbled
2 (15-ounce) cans tomato sauce
1 (14 1/2-ounce) can petite diced tomatoes
1/2 onion, finely chopped
1 (15 1/2-ounce) can red kidney beans
2 (15-ounce) cans black beans
1/4 teaspoon allspice
2 bay leaves
1 teaspoon salt
1/2 teaspoon red pepper
1 1/2 tablespoons chili powder
1 tablespoon vinegar
1 clove garlic, minced
1/4 teaspoon cinnamon

Mix all ingredients together and simmer in a large pan for 1 hour.

✎ **Grocery list:** ground chuck, tomato sauce, petite diced tomatoes, red kidney beans, black beans

✎ **Pantry checklist:** onion, allspice, bay leaves, salt, red pepper, chili powder, vinegar, garlic, cinnamon

Spaghetti Casserole

Yield: 6 servings

1 (26-ounce) jar spaghetti sauce
1 teaspoon brown sugar
1 teaspoon vinegar
salt and pepper to taste
♡1 pound ground chuck, cooked, crumbled, rinsed, and drained
1 teaspoon chili powder
1 clove garlic, minced
1 box angel hair pasta, cooked and drained
♡2 cups shredded cheddar or mozzarella cheese

Preheat oven to 350 degrees.

Mix first 7 ingredients together well and cook on stove top for 30 minutes.

Grease a 9-x-13-inch glass baking dish and place a layer of meat sauce on bottom of dish. Add layer of pasta and 1 cup cheese. Repeat layers, ending with cheese. Bake 20–30 minutes until hot and cheese is melted.

✎ **Grocery list:** spaghetti sauce, ground chuck, pasta, cheddar or mozzarella cheese

✎ **Pantry checklist:** brown sugar, vinegar, salt, pepper, chili powder, garlic

Oven Swiss Steak

Yield: 6 servings

6 pieces cubed steak
1/2 cup and 3 tablespoons flour, divided
1 teaspoon salt
1 teaspoon pepper
1/4 cup vegetable oil
1 (16-ounce) can chopped tomatoes, undrained
1/3 cup chopped celery
1/2 cup thinly sliced carrots
1/2 cup chopped onion

Preheat oven to 350 degrees.

Mix 1/2 cup flour with salt and pepper and dredge steak through it. Brown on both sides in hot oil. Remove from heat and place in greased 9-x-13-inch glass baking dish.

Add 3 tablespoons flour to skillet drippings and heat 1 minute. Add remaining ingredients and cook until mixture begins to thicken. Pour over steak and bake covered 1 1/2 hours.

✎ Grocery list: cubed steak, chopped tomatoes, celery, carrots

✎ Pantry checklist: flour, salt, pepper, vegetable oil, onion

Easy Baked Steak

Yield: 4 servings

4 pieces cubed steak
2–3 tablespoons vegetable oil
♡1 (10 3/4) can cream of mushroom soup
1 soup can water
salt and pepper to taste
1–2 tablespoons Kitchen Bouquet

Preheat oven to 350 degrees.

Brown steak in oil and place in square glass baking dish. Mix soup, water, salt, pepper, and Kitchen Bouquet and heat. Pour over steak and bake covered for 1 1/2 hours.

✎ Grocery list: cubed steak, cream of mushroom soup

✎ Pantry checklist: vegetable oil, salt, pepper, Kitchen Bouquet

Ravioli Lasagna

Yield: 6 servings

1 (10-ounce) package frozen chopped spinach
2 eggs
1 teaspoon salt
½ cup freshly grated Parmesan cheese
1 (32-ounce) jar tomato-basil spaghetti sauce
1 teaspoon brown sugar
1 teaspoon vinegar
♡*1 pound ground chuck, cooked*
1 (24-ounce) package fresh cheese ravioli
♡*2 cups shredded mozzarella cheese, divided*

Preheat oven to 350 degrees.

Thaw spinach for 3½ minutes in the microwave on high and then drain well. Lightly beat eggs in a medium bowl. Add spinach, salt, and Parmesan cheese. In a separate bowl, mix tomato-basil sauce with brown sugar, vinegar, and ground chuck.

Spray 9-x-13-inch glass baking dish with nonstick cooking spray and spread 1 cup tomato-basil-meat mixture on bottom of dish. Add half the ravioli, half the spinach mixture, and then one half of the mozzarella cheese. Repeat layers, topping with remaining 1 cup mozzarella cheese. Bake 30–40 minutes.

✎ **Grocery list:** frozen chopped spinach, Parmesan cheese, spaghetti sauce, ground chuck, fresh cheese ravioli, mozzarella cheese

✎ **Pantry checklist:** eggs, salt, brown sugar, vinegar

> ***Hospitality Note:*** This can be prepared the day before serving. It also freezes well.

Meat Loaf

Yield: 6–8 servings

♡2 *pounds ground chuck*
1 *cup Ritz cracker crumbs or 3 slices white bread, crumbled*
1 *small onion, chopped*
1/2 *green pepper, chopped*
1/2 *cup ketchup or tomato sauce*
1 *tablespoon prepared horseradish*
♡1/4 *cup milk*
2 *large eggs, lightly beaten*
1 *tablespoon Worcestershire sauce*
1 1/2 *teaspoons salt*
1/2 *teaspoon pepper*

Sauce
1/2 *cup ketchup*
1/2 *cup brown sugar*
1 *tablespoon prepared horseradish*
1 *teaspoon brown mustard*

Preheat oven to 350 degrees.

Combine ground chuck with next 10 ingredients. Mix well and place in greased loaf pan.

Combine sauce ingredients in a small bowl and mix well. Spoon half of sauce over meat loaf and bake 1 hour. Spoon remaining sauce over meat loaf and bake 15 more minutes.

✎ **Grocery list:** ground chuck, Ritz crackers or bread, green pepper, horseradish

✎ **Pantry checklist:** onion, ketchup or tomato sauce, milk, eggs, Worcestershire sauce, salt, pepper, brown sugar, brown mustard

Beef Tenderloin with Mushroom Sauce

Yield: 8–10 servings

1 whole beef tenderloin, trimmed

Marinade

1 cup pineapple juice
1 teaspoon ginger
2 cloves garlic, minced
1/3 cup soy sauce
1 teaspoon sugar
♡*1/3 cup olive oil*

Preheat oven to 400 degrees.

Mix marinade ingredients together, pour over the tenderloin, and cover. Marinate the tenderloin overnight in refrigerator. Prior to baking, drain. Bake in a well-greased baking pan 45–60 minutes, depending on how well done you like the meat. Reserve drippings for Mushroom Sauce.

Mushroom Sauce

1 package mushroom gravy mix
1 package brown gravy mix
dash of garlic salt
drippings from tenderloin
2 tablespoons Worcestershire sauce

Prepare gravy mixes according to package directions. Then add garlic salt, drippings from tenderloin, and Worcestershire sauce. Serve with sautéed mushrooms (below) as side dishes.

Sautéed Mushrooms

1/4 cup butter
1 package fresh, whole mushrooms
1/2 cup red cooking wine
1/2 teaspoon garlic salt

Heat skillet and melt butter. Add mushrooms and sauté. Add cooking wine and garlic salt.

✎ **Grocery list:** beef tenderloin, pineapple juice, mushroom gravy mix, brown gravy mix, fresh mushrooms

✎ **Pantry checklist:** ginger, garlic, soy sauce, sugar, olive oil, garlic salt, Worcestershire sauce, butter, red cooking wine

Hospitality Note: You can keep this marinade in the refrigerator; it is delicious on pork, chicken, or beef.

Side Dishes

In the beginning God created the heavens and earth.
—Genesis 1:1

Side dishes make a meal complete since they are usually composed of vegetables, which are so important to our health. I always try to create a menu that includes meat or fish, a green vegetable, salad, fruit, bread, and dessert. Many wonderful vegetable casserole recipes are available, and some can be prepared in advance. Summertime is a great season to visit a farmer's market and prepare a vegetable dinner—fresh green beans, squash, okra, tomatoes, and all that the garden provides.

Summertime is also the source of some of our fondest memories, especially from our vacations in Beaver Creek, Colorado. Our dinner table has been shared with some wonderful people on those trips! Beaver Creek is where we met Joanne and Jack Kemp. I truly enjoy preparing dinner for them and visiting with them. (Joanne always brings a wonderful dessert!) Last year the Kemps brought one of their sons and his family for an evening. It was such fun playing with the little ones and holding them in the swing on the deck as Joanne and I talked.

We have made many special connections in Colorado. I'll never forget meeting the Bernalls the summer after Cassie Bernall was killed in the Columbine school shooting. Michael had just written a song for her, and the family was to hear it for the first time. We shared tears, love, hope, and lunch. Our time together is embedded in my memory. The Bernalls are a special family and are constantly in my thoughts and prayers.

So Colorado summers are filled with rich memories of relationships and shared meals. Just waking up in the morning in Colorado is glorious! I'm usually the first one up, and I love watching the sunrise when everything is quiet. It is such a great place to be reminded of all God has created that is free for us to enjoy—the Beaver Creek as it runs behind the house, the sun on snowcapped mountains just outside the window, the birds, the clouds and sky, family, and good friends. How could anyone not believe in a loving Creator! Colorado is the most beautiful place I have seen.

ROASTED ASPARAGUS

Yield: 6 servings

2 pounds fresh asparagus, trimmed
♡1/4 cup olive oil
1/2 teaspoon salt

Preheat oven to 350 degrees.

Place asparagus in a greased 9-x-13-inch glass baking dish. Drizzle with olive oil and salt. Bake 15 minutes or less, depending on your taste.

✎ **Grocery list:** asparagus
✎ **Pantry checklist:** olive oil, salt

Note: If you like, add fresh sliced mushrooms on either side of the asparagus.

ASPARAGUS AND MUSHROOM CASSEROLE

Yield: 8 servings

3 tablespoons butter
3 tablespoons flour
2 (15-ounce) cans asparagus spears, drained (reserve liquid)
♡1 cup cream or milk
1/2 cup white cooking wine
salt and pepper to taste
dash of cayenne
dash of paprika
♡1/2 cup shredded sharp cheddar cheese
1 (4-ounce) can sliced mushrooms (or use fresh)
2 eggs, hard boiled and sliced
1/2 cup sliced almonds

Preheat oven to 350 degrees.

Melt butter in a medium saucepan. Add flour and blend well. Add liquid from can of asparagus, cream or milk, cooking wine, salt, pepper, cayenne, and paprika. Cook mixture for about 5 minutes. Add cheese and stir until mixture thickens. In a 9-x-13-inch greased baking dish, layer one half of asparagus, mushrooms, sliced eggs, and cream mixture. Repeat layers and sprinkle almonds on top. Bake 30 minutes.

✎ **Grocery list:** asparagus spears, sharp cheddar cheese, sliced mushrooms, almonds
✎ **Pantry checklist:** butter, flour, cream or milk, white cooking wine, salt, pepper, cayenne, paprika, eggs

Cranberry and Pecan Rice

Yield: 8 servings

1 (6-ounce) package long grain wild rice
1 bag boil-in-bag white rice
1/2 cup orange juice
2 tablespoons fresh lemon juice
1 teaspoon salt
1/2 teaspoon pepper
♡*1/2 cup olive oil*
3/4 cup chopped celery
1/4 cup chopped purple onion
2 tablespoons fresh chopped parsley
1 cup dried cranberries
1 cup chopped pecans, toasted

Prepare both packages of rice according to directions. Transfer to a large bowl and fluff with a fork.

Whisk together orange juice, lemon juice, salt, pepper, and olive oil. Pour over rice. Add remaining ingredients; mix well. This can be served cold or hot.

✎ **Grocery list:** long grain wild rice, orange juice, lemon, celery, purple onion, fresh parsley, dried cranberries, pecans

✎ **Pantry checklist:** white rice, salt, pepper, olive oil

Hospitality Note: I prefer serving this hot with Cranberry-Pineapple Pork Tenderloin (see page 110).

SQUASH CASSEROLE

Yield: 6–8 servings

2 pounds yellow squash, sliced
1 small onion, chopped
2 eggs
♡*1 cup crushed saltine crackers*
2 tablespoons butter, melted
1/2 teaspoon salt (more if needed)
1/4 teaspoon pepper
♡*1 cup grated cheddar cheese*
2 tablespoons diced pimiento, drained

Preheat oven to 350 degrees.

Cook squash and onion in salted water until tender. Drain, mash, and add eggs, crackers, butter, salt, pepper, cheese, and pimiento. Bake for 25 minutes.

✎ **Grocery list:** squash, saltine crackers, cheddar cheese, pimientos

✎ **Pantry checklist:** onion, eggs, butter, salt, pepper

ROASTED ZUCCHINI AND YELLOW SQUASH

Yield: 4–6 servings

2 medium zucchini, sliced
2 medium yellow squash, sliced
1 small purple onion, sliced
1 red bell pepper, cut in strips
5 garlic cloves, crushed
♡*2 tablespoons olive oil*
1 teaspoon salt
1/2 teaspoon pepper

Preheat oven to 450 degrees.

Combine first 5 ingredients in a large bowl. Drizzle with oil and sprinkle with salt and pepper. Toss well. Place vegetables on a 15-x-10-inch baking sheet. Bake uncovered 10–20 minutes.

✎ **Grocery list:** zucchini, yellow squash, purple onion, red bell pepper

✎ **Pantry checklist:** garlic, olive oil, salt, pepper

Squash and Dressing Casserole

Yield: 8 servings

3 tablespoons butter, melted
1 cup herb-seasoned stuffing mix
2 pounds squash, cooked and drained
1 onion, chopped
♡*1 can cream of chicken soup*
♡*1 cup shredded cheddar cheese*
1/4 cup diced pimiento, drained
♡*1 cup sour cream*
2 eggs, lightly beaten
1 teaspoon salt
1/2 teaspoon baking powder

Preheat oven to 350 degrees.

Mix butter and stuffing mix. In a separate bowl, mix half of stuffing-butter combination with remaining ingredients and spoon into greased 9-x-13-inch glass baking dish. Top with remaining stuffing-butter mix and bake 30–40 minutes.

✎ **Grocery list:** herb-seasoned stuffing mix, squash, cream of chicken soup, cheddar cheese, pimientos, sour cream
✎ **Pantry checklist:** butter, onion, eggs, salt, baking powder

Hospitality Note: This casserole can be prepared a day in advance and baked the day of serving.

Corn Pudding

Yield: 6 servings

6 ears corn, cut from cob, or 2 (10-ounce) packages frozen corn, thawed
3 tablespoons flour
1/2 cup sugar
1 teaspoon baking powder
salt to taste
2 tablespoons butter, melted
3 eggs
♡*1 cup milk*

Preheat oven to 350 degrees.

Mix all ingredients together and pour into greased 1 1/2 quart baking dish. Bake 30–40 minutes or until set.

✎ **Grocery list:** corn
✎ **Pantry checklist:** flour, sugar, baking powder, salt, butter, eggs, milk

CARROT SOUFFLÉ

Yield: 6 servings

1 pound carrots, peeled and chopped
3 large eggs, separated
1/2 cup sugar
1/3 cup butter, melted
3 tablespoons flour
1 teaspoon baking powder
1 teaspoon vanilla
1/4 teaspoon nutmeg

Preheat oven to 350 degrees.

Cover carrots in saucepan with water and cook 45 minutes or until very tender. Drain and purée in food processor. Mix carrot purée, egg yolks, sugar, butter, flour, baking powder, vanilla, and nutmeg. Beat egg whites until soft peaks form; fold into carrot mixture. Spoon into greased 9-x-13-inch baking dish and bake 45 minutes or until set.

✎ **Grocery list:** carrots

✎ **Pantry checklist:** eggs, sugar, butter, flour, baking powder, vanilla, nutmeg

SWEET POTATOES WITH APRICOT GLAZE

Yield: 8 servings

6 medium sweet potatoes, cooked and peeled
1/4 cup butter
1/2 cup brown sugar
1/2 cup apricot preserves
1 teaspoon nutmeg
1/2 cup chopped pecans, toasted

Preheat oven to 350 degrees.

Slice sweet potatoes and place in 9-x-13-inch lightly greased dish. Combine butter, brown sugar, and apricot preserves in a small saucepan and heat until well mixed. Pour over sweet potatoes and sprinkle with nutmeg and pecans. Bake 30 minutes or until well heated.

✎ **Grocery list:** sweet potatoes, apricot preserves, pecans

✎ **Pantry checklist:** butter, brown sugar, nutmeg

Sweet Potato Casserole

Yield: 6–8 servings

3 cups cooked and mashed sweet potatoes
1/4 cup melted butter
1/2 cup sugar
1 teaspoon vanilla

Topping

1 cup light brown sugar
1/3 cup flour
1/3 cup butter, softened
1 cup chopped pecans

Preheat oven to 350 degrees.

Blend sweet potatoes, butter, sugar, and vanilla together in mixer. Spoon into 9-x-13-inch greased casserole dish.

Mix together the topping ingredients and sprinkle on top of sweet potatoes. Bake 30 minutes.

✎ **Grocery list:** sweet potatoes, pecans
✎ **Pantry checklist:** butter, sugar, vanilla, brown sugar, flour

> ***Hospitality Note:*** This casserole can be prepared a day in advance and baked on the day of serving.

BUTTER BEANS

Yield: 6 servings

2 (10-ounce) packages frozen butter beans
♡4 slices bacon
2 green onions, chopped
1 clove garlic, minced
1/2 cup fresh parsley, chopped
1/2 teaspoon salt
1/2 teaspoon pepper

Cook butter beans according to directions and set aside. Cook bacon crisp and drain on paper towel. Add onions and garlic to bacon drippings and cook until tender. Combine all ingredients except for the bacon and cook just until heated. Top with bacon.

Grocery list: butter beans, bacon, green onions, fresh parsley
Pantry checklist: garlic, salt, pepper

GREEN BEANS

Yield: 8 servings

2 (28-ounce) cans green beans
2 teaspoons salt
1/4 cup sugar
2 tablespoons vegetable oil
2 tablespoons butter
1 tablespoon chopped onion

Drain liquid from beans; place in a large pan and add about a cup of water to half cover beans. Add remaining ingredients. Cover and cook on medium-high heat for 20 minutes; then reduce heat to low and cook for 1 1/2 hours.

✎ **Grocery list:** green beans
✎ **Pantry checklist:** salt, sugar, vegetable oil, butter, onion

Baked Beans

Yield: 8 servings

1 medium onion, chopped
3 (16-ounce) cans pork and beans
1 (12-ounce) jar chili sauce
1 (8-ounce) can crushed pineapple, drained
3/4 cup brown sugar
1 tablespoon dry mustard
1 tablespoon Worcestershire sauce

Preheat oven to 350 degrees.

Combine all ingredients and mix well. Spoon into greased 9-x-13-inch baking dish and bake 1 hour.

✎ **Grocery list:** pork and beans, chili sauce, crushed pineapple

✎ **Pantry checklist:** onion, brown sugar, dry mustard, Worcestershire sauce

Creamy Orzo with Sautéed Spinach

Yield: 4–5 servings

1 cup dry orzo pasta, cooked and drained but not rinsed
1/4 cup freshly grated Parmesan cheese
♡2 tablespoons cream
salt and pepper to taste
1 pound fresh spinach, stemmed
♡2 tablespoons olive oil
3–4 garlic cloves, thinly sliced
salt and pepper to taste

Mix orzo, Parmesan cheese, cream, salt, and pepper together and set aside.

Sauté spinach in olive oil with garlic, salt, and pepper for only a minute or two. Place orzo on platter and top with spinach.

✎ **Grocery list:** orzo pasta, Parmesan cheese, cream, fresh spinach

✎ **Pantry checklist:** salt, pepper, olive oil, garlic

SPINACH-ARTICHOKE CASSEROLE

Yield: 8 servings

1 (14-ounce) can artichoke hearts, drained and coarsely chopped
1 (10-ounce) package frozen chopped spinach
1/2 cup chopped onion
1/3 cup butter, melted
♡*1/2 cup sour cream*
3/4 cup freshly grated Parmesan cheese, divided
3/4 teaspoon salt
3/4 teaspoon white pepper
dash of red pepper

Preheat oven to 350 degrees.

Arrange artichoke hearts in a lightly greased 9-x-13-inch baking dish.

Thaw spinach for 3 1/2 minutes in the microwave on high; then drain well and set aside. Cook onion in butter in a large skillet until tender. Stir in spinach, sour cream, 1/4 cup Parmesan cheese, salt, white pepper, and red pepper. Spoon spinach mixture over artichokes and top with 1/2 cup Parmesan cheese.

Bake 25–30 minutes or until thoroughly heated.

✎ **Grocery list:** artichoke hearts, frozen spinach, sour cream, Parmesan cheese

✎ **Pantry checklist:** onion, butter, salt, white pepper, red pepper

SPINACH SOUFFLÉ

Yield: 4–5 servings

1 (10-ounce) package frozen spinach
3 eggs, beaten
1/2 teaspoon salt
2 tablespoons flour
1/4 cup butter, melted
♡*1 cup small-curd cottage cheese*
♡*1 1/2 cups shredded cheddar cheese*

Preheat oven to 350 degrees.

Thaw spinach for 3 1/2 minutes in the microwave on high and then drain well. Mix spinach with remaining ingredients until well blended. Spoon into a round baking dish and bake 30–40 minutes or until set.

✎ **Grocery list:** frozen spinach, small-curd cottage cheese, cheddar cheese

✎ **Pantry checklist:** eggs, salt, flour, butter

Hash-Brown Casserole

Yield: 8 servings

1 (32-ounce) package hash-brown potatoes, thawed
♡2 cups shredded cheddar cheese
1/4 cup butter, melted
♡1 1/2 cups sour cream
3 green onions, thinly sliced
1/2 teaspoon garlic salt
1/2 teaspoon salt
1/4 teaspoon pepper
♡1 (10 3/4-ounce) can cream of chicken soup

Topping

2 cups crushed cornflakes
3 tablespoons butter, melted

Preheat oven to 350 degrees.

Mix hash browns with next 8 ingredients and place in greased 9-x-13-inch casserole dish.

Mix cornflakes and 3 tablespoons butter and place on top of hash-brown mixture. Bake 40 minutes or until done.

✎ **Grocery list:** hash-brown potatoes, cheddar cheese, sour cream, green onions, cream of chicken soup, cornflakes

✎ **Pantry checklist:** butter, garlic salt, salt, pepper

Herbed New Potatoes

Yield: 6 servings

2 pounds red new potatoes, cut in half
2 tablespoons butter, melted
2 tablespoons chopped parsley
2 tablespoons chopped chives
salt and pepper to taste

Steam potatoes until fully cooked. Toss potatoes with the remaining ingredients.

Serve hot!

✎ **Grocery list:** red new potatoes

✎ **Pantry checklist:** butter, parsley, chives, salt, pepper

AU GRATIN POTATOES

Yield: 12–15 servings

1/2 cup butter
1/2 cup flour
♡*1 (14-ounce) can chicken broth*
♡*1/2 cup cream or milk*
1 garlic clove, minced
salt and pepper to taste
dash of cayenne
1 teaspoon dry mustard
♡*2 cups shredded sharp cheddar cheese*
5 pounds potatoes, peeled, cooked, and sliced
paprika

Preheat oven to 350 degrees.

Melt butter and add flour, stirring until well mixed. Add chicken broth and cream or milk and cook until mixture begins to thicken. Add garlic, salt, pepper, cayenne, dry mustard, and cheese. Continue to stir on medium heat until cheese is well blended.

Place one layer of sliced potatoes in greased 9-x-13-inch dish and add layer of cheese sauce. Repeat this procedure two more times. Sprinkle with paprika and bake 30 minutes.

✎ **Grocery list:** chicken broth, sharp cheddar cheese, potatoes

✎ **Pantry checklist:** butter, flour, cream or milk, garlic, salt, pepper, cayenne, dry mustard, paprika

Sour Cream Potatoes

Yield: 10–12 servings

6 large baking potatoes
1/4 cup butter
2 green onions, chopped
1/2 teaspoon dry mustard
1 teaspoon salt
♡*2 cups sour cream*
♡*1 1/2 cups shredded cheddar cheese*

Topping

1/4 cup butter
1 1/2 cups cornflakes, finely crushed

Preheat oven to 350 degrees.

Cook potatoes until tender. Drain and refrigerate. Shred cooled potatoes in a food processor and mix with 1/4 cup butter, green onions, dry mustard, salt, sour cream, and cheese. Spoon into greased 9-x-13-inch baking dish. For topping, mix 1/4 cup butter and cornflake crumbs together and sprinkle on potatoes. Bake 30 minutes.

✎ **Grocery list:** baking potatoes, green onions, sour cream, cheddar cheese, cornflakes

✎ **Pantry checklist:** butter, dry mustard, salt

Mashed Potato Casserole

Yield: 6 servings

1 (22-ounce) package frozen mashed potatoes
♡*4 ounces cream cheese, room temperature*
♡*1/2 cup sour cream*
1 green onion, finely sliced
1/4 teaspoon garlic salt
1/2 teaspoon pepper
♡*1/2 cup shredded cheddar cheese*

Preheat oven to 350 degrees.

Prepare potatoes according to package directions. Stir in cream cheese, sour cream, green onion, garlic salt, and pepper. Spoon into a greased casserole dish and top with cheddar cheese. Bake 20 minutes or until thoroughly heated.

✎ **Grocery list:** frozen mashed potatoes, cream cheese, sour cream, green onions, cheddar cheese

✎ **Pantry checklist:** garlic salt, pepper

BROCCOLI-RITZ CASSEROLE

Yield: 6–7 servings

2 (10-ounce) packages frozen broccoli florets
♡*2 tablespoons milk*
♡*1 cup shredded cheddar cheese*
24 Ritz crackers, crushed
1/4 cup butter, melted

Preheat oven to 350 degrees.

Cook broccoli until tender but still crisp. Don't overcook. Drain and place in 9-x-13-inch greased baking dish. Pour milk over broccoli and top with cheese. Mix Ritz crackers with butter and sprinkle on top of cheese. Bake 20–25 minutes.

✎ **Grocery list:** broccoli florets, cheddar cheese, Ritz crackers
✎ **Pantry checklist:** milk, butter

BROCCOLI SOUFFLÉ

Yield: 4–5 servings

1 (10-ounce) package frozen chopped broccoli
♡*1 cup cottage cheese*
3 eggs, beaten
2 tablespoons flour
1/2 teaspoon salt
1/4 cup butter, melted
♡*1 cup shredded sharp cheddar cheese*

Preheat oven to 350 degrees.

Cook broccoli according to microwave directions and drain well. Mix broccoli with remaining ingredients and spoon into a greased round or square baking dish. Bake 40 minutes.

✎ **Grocery list:** frozen chopped broccoli, cottage cheese, sharp cheddar cheese
✎ **Pantry checklist:** eggs, flour, salt, butter

Peas Amandine

Yield: 6–7 servings

1 (16-ounce) package frozen peas
3 tablespoons butter
1/4 cup slivered almonds
1/4 cup chopped onion
1 (4 1/2-ounce) jar sliced mushrooms, drained
1 teaspoon salt
1/8 teaspoon pepper

Cook peas according to package directions; drain. Set aside and keep warm. Melt butter in skillet and sauté almonds until lightly browned. Remove with slotted spoon and add to peas. In same skillet, sauté onion and mushrooms. Add to peas and season with salt and pepper.

✎ **Grocery list:** frozen peas, almonds, sliced mushrooms

✎ **Pantry checklist:** butter, onion, salt, pepper

SWEETS

By wisdom a house is built,
and through understanding it is established;
through knowledge its rooms are filled
with rare and beautiful treasures.
—PROVERBS 24:3–4

Cakes, frozen pies, pastry crusts, muffins, and cookies are easily prepared and frozen in advance for last-minute occasions. I keep many of these items in my freezer at all times. I also keep frosting in the refrigerator.

Sweets is a much-loved word with my grandchildren. My kitchen is a sea of sugar as we bake and decorate birthday cakes and make cookies—and eat the cookie dough and frosting! Spending time with my grandchildren is such a blessing. From the time they were born, I've had a special bond with them—they are truly a gift from God. I know that the most precious gift I can give them is my unconditional love, my time, my wisdom, and my values.

I am blessed to live near my grandchildren and to be involved in their lives. They already are learning the meaning of hospitality. Whitney leads a Bible study for young girls at her church and enjoys entertaining them at her home. She is the master decorator as we bake cookies and cakes. Emily and Anna are involved in the ministry Family Affair, which helps

families who are less fortunate. Together we have made cookies, fudge sauce, and preserves for gifts. Mary Claire and Caroline love to help me prepare meals, set the table, and clean up. I am proud of my grandsons, Ryan and Tyler, as well and am amazed at their compassion for those with less. Ryan has a ministry with the homeless; Tyler takes care of the children in the nursery at church.

And I'll never forget when Sarah Kate (who was four years old at the time) was watching me fix pigs-in-a-blanket one day after baking Christmas cookies together. As I was wrapping the wieners in dough, she turned to her cousins and said, "Look! Mimi is wrapping the wieners in swaddling clothes just like Jesus!"

I mentioned earlier in the book that I taught a hospitality-cooking class at Belmont. I arrived early that evening and was met by three young ladies waiting to greet me. One of the girls had just picked up her mail. Inside a package from her grandmother was a Pringles can filled with homemade cookies. She said her grandmother sends her cookies and quarters when she can. We were all moved to tears by her letter and gift. Many thoughts went through my mind at that moment. It reminded me that no matter how little or much we have, we need to share with others.

And my next thought was, *I want to be remembered like her grandmother.* I want my grandchildren to think of me with fondness and love. I hope they think of the little things I do for them and the time I spend with them and my prayers for them. My daily prayer for my grandchildren is that God would place His loving arms and guardian angels around them to protect them and that they would grow up to be whole—mentally, physically, emotionally, and most of all spiritually.

As we match our words with actions, we can make a profound and lasting impression on the generations to come.

PECAN PIE

Yield: 6–7 servings

1/3 cup butter, room temperature
1/2 cup brown sugar
1/2 cup granulated sugar
1 tablespoon flour
4 large eggs
♡1 cup corn syrup
1/4 teaspoon salt
1 teaspoon vanilla
1 1/2 cups chopped pecans
1 (9-inch) piecrust, unbaked

Preheat oven to 325 degrees.

Beat butter at medium speed in mixer until creamy. Add brown and granulated sugars and flour, beating until well mixed. Add eggs, 1 at a time, mixing well after each addition. Add corn syrup, salt, and vanilla and mix thoroughly. Stir in chopped pecans and pour into piecrust. Bake 50 minutes or until set.

✎ **Grocery list:** pecans, piecrust

✎ **Pantry checklist:** butter, brown sugar, granulated sugar, flour, eggs, corn syrup, salt, vanilla

CHOCOLATE PECAN PIE

Yield: 7–8 servings

4 large eggs
♡1 cup corn syrup
6 tablespoons butter, melted
1/2 cup sugar
1/4 cup brown sugar
1 tablespoon vanilla
1 tablespoon flour
1/2 cup semisweet chocolate chips, melted
1 cup chopped pecans
1 (9-inch) piecrust, unbaked
♡ice cream or whipped topping, to serve

Preheat oven to 350 degrees.

Whisk together eggs and next 6 ingredients until blended; stir in melted chocolate and pecans, and pour into piecrust.

Bake on lowest rack for 1 hour. Place foil around piecrust after 20 minutes to keep pie from browning too much. Cool completely. Serve with ice cream or whipped topping.

✎ **Grocery list:** semisweet chocolate chips, pecans, piecrust, ice cream or whipped topping

✎ **Pantry checklist:** eggs, corn syrup, butter, sugar, brown sugar, vanilla, flour

Pumpkin-Pecan Pie

Yield: 6–7 servings

Pumpkin Layer

1 cup canned pumpkin
1/3 cup sugar
1 large egg
1 teaspoon pumpkin pie spice
1 (9-inch) deep-dish piecrust, unbaked

Preheat oven to 350 degrees.

Mix all ingredients together well and spread in piecrust.

Pecan Layer

♡2/3 cup corn syrup
1/2 cup sugar
2 large eggs
3 tablespoons butter, melted
1/2 teaspoon vanilla
1 cup pecans, chopped or whole

Mix corn syrup, sugar, eggs, butter, and vanilla and mix well. Pour over pumpkin layer. Top with pecans. Bake 50 minutes or until set.

✎ **Grocery list:** canned pumpkin, piecrust, pecans

✎ **Pantry checklist:** sugar, eggs, pumpkin pie spice, corn syrup, butter, vanilla

Sweet Potato and Pecan Pie with Cinnamon Cream

Yield: 6–7 servings

1 pound (or 2 medium) sweet potatoes, baked, peeled, and warm
1/4 cup butter
♡*1 (14-ounce) can sweetened condensed milk*
1 teaspoon vanilla
1 teaspoon cinnamon
1 teaspoon nutmeg
1/4 teaspoon salt
2 eggs, beaten
1 (9-inch) deep-dish piecrust, unbaked

Preheat oven to 350 degrees.

In a large mixing bowl, beat warm sweet potatoes with butter until smooth. Add condensed milk, vanilla, cinnamon, nutmeg, salt, and eggs and mix well. Pour into piecrust.

Topping

1 egg
3 tablespoons dark corn syrup
3 tablespoons brown sugar
1 tablespoon butter, melted
1 cup chopped pecans

Combine egg, corn syrup, brown sugar, and butter. Mix well and add pecans. Spoon over pie and bake 20–25 minutes.

Cinnamon Cream

♡*1 (8-ounce) container frozen whipped topping, thawed*
1/2 teaspoon cinnamon

Mix together and use to garnish the pie.

✎ **Grocery list:** sweet potatoes, condensed milk, piecrust, pecans, whipped topping
✎ **Pantry checklist:** butter, vanilla, cinnamon, nutmeg, salt, eggs, dark corn syrup, brown sugar

Cream Cheese Pecan Pie

Yield: 7–8 servings

♡1 (8-ounce) package cream cheese, room temperature
4 large eggs, divided
3/4 cup sugar, divided
1/4 teaspoon salt
2 teaspoons vanilla, divided
1 (9-inch) piecrust, unbaked
1 cup chopped pecans
♡1 cup corn syrup
2 tablespoons butter, melted

Preheat oven to 350 degrees.

Mix cream cheese, 1 egg, 1/2 cup sugar, salt, and 1 teaspoon vanilla in mixer until well blended. Pour into piecrust and top with pecans. Stir together corn syrup, 1/4 cup sugar, 1 teaspoon vanilla, remaining 3 eggs, and butter and pour over pecans. Bake 50–55 minutes or until set.

✎ **Grocery list:** cream cheese, piecrust, pecans
✎ **Pantry checklist:** eggs, sugar, salt, vanilla, corn syrup, butter

Strawberry Cream Cheese Pie

Yield: 12 servings

♡1 (8-ounce) package cream cheese, room temperature
1/2 cup sugar
♡1 (12-ounce) container frozen whipped topping, thawed
4 cups chopped fresh strawberries
2 Oreo piecrusts

Beat cream cheese and sugar together until well blended. Add whipped topping and mix well. Fold in strawberries. Place in the 2 piecrusts and freeze. Prior to serving, remove from freezer to thaw for a few minutes. Garnish with fresh strawberry.

✎ **Grocery list:** cream cheese, whipped topping, fresh strawberries, Oreo piecrusts
✎ **Pantry checklist:** sugar

> ***Hospitality Note:*** Not only is this an easy dessert to make, it's a great dessert to keep in the freezer for last-minute occasions. Also, I once substituted a 10-ounce package of frozen raspberries for the strawberries, and it was great!

CHOCOLATE CREAM CHEESE PIE

Yield: 12 servings

♡1 *(8-ounce) package cream cheese, room temperature*
1/2 cup sugar
3 (1-ounce) squares semisweet chocolate, melted
1/8 teaspoon almond flavoring
♡2 *(12-ounce) containers frozen whipped topping, thawed*
1 (8-ounce) package chocolate-covered toffee bits, divided
2 Oreo piecrusts

Mix cream cheese and sugar together in mixer; add melted chocolate and almond flavoring. Add whipped topping, mixing well, and fold in all but 1/8 cup of chocolate-covered toffee bits. Spread into piecrusts and refrigerate. Garnish with remaining toffee bits.

✎ **Grocery list:** cream cheese, semisweet chocolate, whipped topping, chocolate-covered toffee bits, Oreo piecrusts
✎ **Pantry checklist:** sugar, almond flavoring

LEMON PIE

Yield: 6–7 servings

1 1/4 cups sugar
1/2 cup cornstarch
1/4 teaspoon salt
4 large egg yolks
2 cups water
1/2 cup fresh lemon juice
4 tablespoons butter
2 teaspoons grated lemon rind
1 (9-inch) piecrust, baked
♡1 *(8-ounce) container frozen whipped topping, thawed*

Combine sugar, cornstarch, and salt in saucepan. Mix egg yolks with water using whisk and add to sugar mix. Cook on medium heat until mixture thickens. Stir in lemon juice, butter, and lemon rind and mix well. Remove from heat and pour into crust. Cool; then refrigerate. Prior to serving, top with whipped topping.

✎ **Grocery list:** lemons, piecrust, whipped topping
✎ **Pantry checklist:** sugar, cornstarch, salt, eggs, butter

Toffee Bits Cream Pie

Yield: 6–7 servings

♡$2\frac{1}{2}$ *cups milk*
3 egg yolks
1 cup sugar
$\frac{1}{8}$ *teaspoon salt*
$4\frac{1}{2}$ *tablespoons cornstarch*
1 teaspoon vanilla
2 tablespoons butter
1 (9-inch) deep-dish piecrust, baked
$\frac{3}{4}$ *cup chocolate-covered toffee bits, divided*
♡*whipping cream or whipped topping*

Combine milk and egg yolks, mixing well. In a medium saucepan mix sugar, salt, and cornstarch with whisk. Add milk-egg mixture and cook over medium heat until thickened. Remove from heat and stir in vanilla and butter.

Place half of pie filling in cooled piecrust and top with $\frac{1}{4}$ cup toffee bits; add remaining pie filling and put another $\frac{1}{4}$ cup toffee bits on top. Place in refrigerator until cool. Top with whipping cream or whipped topping. Garnish with remaining toffee bits.

✎ **Grocery list:** piecrust, chocolate-covered toffee bits, whipping cream or whipped topping

✎ **Pantry checklist:** milk, eggs, sugar, salt, cornstarch, vanilla, butter

BANANA-TOFFEE CREAM PIE

Yield: 6–7 servings

1 cup sugar
4 tablespoons cornstarch
1/8 teaspoon salt
♡*2 1/2 cups milk*
3 egg yolks
2 tablespoons butter
1 teaspoon vanilla
3/4 cup chocolate-covered toffee bits, divided
2 bananas, sliced, divided
1 (9-inch) piecrust, baked
♡*whipping cream or whipped topping, to serve*

Combine sugar, cornstarch, and salt in saucepan. Blend milk and egg yolks together in a separate bowl and add to sugar mixture. Cook over medium heat until mixture thickens. Remove from heat. Add butter and vanilla.

Place half of cream pie filling in crust and top with 1/4 cup toffee bits and 1 sliced banana. Add remaining pie filling and another 1/4 cup toffee bits and top with 1 sliced banana. Place in refrigerator until cool. Top with whipping cream or whipped topping. Garnish with remaining toffee bits.

✎ **Grocery list:** chocolate-covered toffee bits, bananas, piecrust, whipping cream or whipped topping

✎ **Pantry checklist:** sugar, cornstarch, salt, milk, eggs, butter, vanilla

CHOCOLATE CREAM PIE

Yield: 6–7 servings

♡2 1/2 *cups milk*
3 *egg yolks*
1 *cup sugar*
1/8 *teaspoon salt*
1/4 *cup cocoa*
4 1/2 *tablespoons cornstarch*
1/4 *teaspoon almond flavoring*
1 *tablespoon butter*
1 *(9-inch) piecrust, baked*

Combine milk and egg yolks, mixing well. In a medium saucepan, mix sugar, salt, cocoa, and cornstarch with whisk. Add milk-egg mixture and cook over medium heat until thickened. Remove from heat and stir in almond flavoring and butter. Spoon into cooled crust.

Meringue

3 *egg whites*
1/4 *teaspoon cream of tartar*
1/3 *cup sugar*
2 *tablespoons marshmallow cream*
1/2 *teaspoon vanilla*

Preheat oven to 325 degrees.

Beat egg whites with cream of tartar in mixer until soft peaks form. Gradually add sugar, beating at high speed until stiff peaks form. Fold in marshmallow cream and vanilla and blend well. Spread meringue over pie filling, sealing to edge of pastry. Bake 15–20 minutes or until browned.

✎ **Grocery list:** piecrust, marshmallow cream
✎ **Pantry checklist:** milk, eggs, sugar, salt, cocoa, cornstarch, almond flavoring, butter, cream of tartar, vanilla

> *Hospitality Note:* You can use whipped topping instead of meringue. Garnish with fresh strawberries.

Coconut Cream Pie

Yield: 6–7 servings

1 cup sugar
4 1/2 tablespoons cornstarch
1/8 teaspoon salt
♡2 1/2 cups milk
3 egg yolks
2 tablespoons butter
1 teaspoon vanilla
1/2 cup shredded coconut
1 (9-inch) piecrust, baked

Mix sugar, cornstarch, and salt in saucepan. In a medium bowl, combine milk and egg yolks and mix with whisk. Gradually add to sugar mixture. Cook on medium heat, stirring constantly, until mixture thickens. Remove from heat and add butter, vanilla, and coconut. Spoon into cooled piecrust.

Meringue

3 egg whites
1/4 teaspoon cream of tartar
1/3 cup sugar
2 tablespoons marshmallow cream
1/2 teaspoon vanilla

Preheat oven to 325 degrees.

Beat egg whites with cream of tartar in mixer until soft peaks form. Gradually add sugar, beating at high speed until stiff peaks form. Fold in marshmallow cream and vanilla and blend well. Spread meringue over pie filling, sealing to edge of pastry. Bake 15–20 minutes or until browned.

✎ **Grocery list:** coconut, piecrust, marshmallow cream or whipped topping
✎ **Pantry checklist:** sugar, cornstarch, salt, milk, eggs, butter, vanilla, cream of tartar

Note: You can also use whipped topping instead of the meringue.

Hospitality Note: Place 1/4 cup coconut in microwave and heat just until lightly browned. Top pie with toasted coconut.

Lemon Angel Pie with Raspberry Sauce

Yield: 24 servings

Meringue

12 large eggs, separated
1 1/2 teaspoons cream of tartar
3 cups sugar
1/2 teaspoon salt
1 1/2 tablespoons vanilla

Preheat oven to 250 degrees.

Beat egg whites and cream of tartar until stiff. Gradually add sugar, salt, and vanilla and beat until sugar is dissolved. Place mixture in 2 greased 9-x-13-inch glass baking dishes. Bake 1 hour. Cool completely.

Filling

12 egg yolks
5 tablespoons hot water
grated rind of 1 lemon
3/4 cup sugar
juice of 2 lemons
2 pints whipping cream

Combine ingredients in double boiler and cook until thick. After mixture cools, place thin layer of lemon filling on top of each dish of meringue. Cover and refrigerate overnight. When ready to serve, whip the whipping cream and spread on top of each meringue.

Raspberry Sauce

3 tablespoons flour
1/2 cup sugar
1 (10-ounce) package frozen raspberries
1 pint fresh raspberries for garnish

Mix flour, sugar, and frozen raspberries in a small saucepan. Cook until it begins to thicken. This will be a thin sauce. Cool.

When ready to serve angel pie, cut into squares and place on plate. Drizzle with raspberry sauce and put 2 or 3 fresh raspberries on top.

✎ **Grocery list:** lemons, whipping cream, frozen raspberries, fresh raspberries
✎ **Pantry checklist:** eggs, cream of tartar, sugar, salt, vanilla, flour

Note: You can substitute 2 (11 1/2-ounce) jars of lemon curd for this filling.

COCONUT-PINEAPPLE CHESS PIE

Yield: 7–8 servings

1 1/2 cups sugar

3 tablespoons cornmeal

2 tablespoons flour

1/4 teaspoon salt

4 large eggs, lightly beaten

1 teaspoon vanilla

1/4 cup butter, melted

2 cups crushed pineapple, drained

1 (3 1/2-ounce) can flaked coconut

1 (9-inch) piecrust, unbaked

♡whipped topping, to serve

Preheat oven to 350 degrees.

Combine first 4 ingredients in a large bowl. Add eggs and vanilla, stirring until blended. Add butter, pineapple, and coconut. Pour into piecrust and bake 1 hour or until set. Cool and serve with whipping topping.

✎ **Grocery list:** crushed pineapple, coconut, piecrust, whipped topping

✎ **Pantry checklist:** sugar, cornmeal, flour, salt, eggs, vanilla, butter

CHOCOLATE CHESS PIE

Yield: 6–7 servings

1 1/2 cups sugar

3 1/2 tablespoons cocoa

2 tablespoons flour

1 stick butter, room temperature

2 eggs

1/8 teaspoon salt

♡1 small (3/4 cup) can evaporated milk

1 teaspoon vanilla

1 (9-inch) piecrust, unbaked

♡whipped topping and grated chocolate, to serve

Preheat oven to 400 degrees.

Mix sugar, cocoa, flour, and butter. Cream well and add eggs; beat with mixer for 2 minutes. Add salt, milk, and vanilla. Pour filling into unbaked piecrust and bake 10 minutes. Reduce temperature to 325 degrees and bake for another 35–45 minutes or until set. Cool and serve with whipped topping and grated chocolate. Very rich and delicious!

✎ **Grocery list:** evaporated milk, piecrust, whipped topping, chocolate squares

✎ **Pantry checklist:** sugar, cocoa, flour, butter, eggs, salt, vanilla

Caramel Apple Pie

Yield: 6–7 servings

1/2 cup sugar
3 tablespoons flour
1 teaspoon ground cinnamon
1/2 teaspoon nutmeg
1/8 teaspoon salt
6 cups thinly sliced Granny Smith apples, peeled
1 (9-inch) deep-dish piecrust, unbaked

In a large mixing bowl, stir together sugar, flour, cinnamon, nutmeg, and salt. Add apples and gently toss until coated. Place apple mixture in pie shell. Top pie with crumb topping.

Crumb Topping

1 cup brown sugar
1/2 cup flour
1/2 cup quick-cooking oats
1/2 cup butter

Preheat oven to 375 degrees.

Stir together brown sugar, flour, and oats. Cut in butter until topping is crumb consistency. Spoon topping on top of apples. Bake 50–60 minutes. Remove from oven.

Caramel Topping

1/3 cup caramel topping
1/2 cup chopped pecans, toasted

Drizzle pie with caramel topping and chopped pecans.

✎ **Grocery list:** apples, piecrust, quick-cooking oats, caramel topping, pecans

✎ **Pantry checklist:** granulated sugar, flour, cinnamon, nutmeg, salt, brown sugar, butter

EASY ICE CREAM PIE

Yield: 6–7 servings

♡½ *gallon vanilla ice cream*
1 *cup chocolate syrup*
1 *cup caramel topping*
1 *package chocolate-covered toffee bits*

Piecrust
1 *cup grape nuts cereal*
1 *cup multibran Chex cereal*
¼ *cup powdered sugar*
¼ *cup butter, softened*

Pulse piecrust ingredients in food processor until fine. Press into 9-inch pie pan.

Let ice cream soften 10 minutes. Spread one layer of ice cream in piecrust; drizzle with half of the chocolate syrup and half the caramel topping and sprinkle with a layer of toffee bits. Repeat layers and freeze.

✎ **Grocery list:** ice cream, chocolate syrup, caramel topping, chocolate-covered toffee bits, grape nuts cereal, multibran Chex cereal, powdered sugar

✎ **Pantry checklist:** butter

Note: You can vary the kinds of ice cream and toppings.

LOW-FAT PEANUT BUTTER PIE

Yield: 6–7 servings

4 *ounces fat-free cream cheese, room temperature*
1 *(8-ounce) container light whipped topping, thawed*
3 *heaping tablespoons fat-free peanut butter*
12 *packets sweetener*
1 *graham-cracker piecrust*

Mix together cream cheese, whipped topping, peanut butter, and sweetener. Spoon into graham-cracker crust. Freeze.

✎ **Grocery list:** fat-free cream cheese, light whipped topping, fat-free peanut butter, sweetener, graham-cracker piecrust

Peach Cobbler

Yield: 6–7 servings

4 cups sliced fresh peaches, peeled
1 cup sugar
3–4 tablespoons flour
1 tablespoon butter
1/4 teaspoon nutmeg
1 (9-inch) piecrust, unbaked
♡ *vanilla ice cream, to serve*

Preheat oven to 400 degrees.

Mix first 3 ingredients in saucepan and cook until peaches are tender. Remove from heat and add butter and nutmeg. Place mixture in 8-inch square baking dish and top with piecrust (roll to fit dish). Bake 20–30 minutes or until crust has browned. Serve with vanilla ice cream.

✎ **Grocery list:** fresh peaches, piecrust, ice cream

✎ **Pantry checklist:** sugar, flour, butter, nutmeg

Blackberry Cobbler

Yield: 8 servings

2 (16-ounce) packages frozen blackberries, thawed
1 cup sugar
3 tablespoons flour
3/4 cup water
1 tablespoon lemon juice
1 (9-inch) piecrust, unbaked
2 tablespoons butter, melted

Preheat oven to 400 degrees.

Spread berries in a lightly greased 9-x-13-inch baking dish. In a small bowl, combine sugar and flour and stir in water and lemon juice. Pour mixture over berries. Top with piecrust (roll to fit dish) and brush with butter. Bake 30 minutes or until crust is golden brown.

✎ **Grocery list:** blackberries, piecrust

✎ **Pantry checklist:** sugar, flour, lemon juice, butter

CHOCOLATE CARAMEL DELIGHT

Yield: 6–7 servings

3 egg whites
1 cup sugar, less 3 tablespoons
3/4 teaspoon vanilla
1 cup chopped pecans
20 Ritz crackers, crushed
butter
♡*1 (8-ounce) container frozen whipped topping, thawed*
caramel topping
chocolate syrup

Preheat oven to 350 degrees.

Beat egg whites until stiff. Add sugar gradually, then vanilla. Fold in nuts and crackers and pour into buttered 9-inch pie plate. Bake 30–35 minutes. Cool and then spread with whipped topping. Drizzle with butterscotch topping and chocolate syrup.

✎ **Grocery list:** pecans, Ritz crackers, whipped topping, butterscotch topping, chocolate syrup

✎ **Pantry checklist:** eggs, sugar, vanilla, butter

EASY FLAKY PASTRY

Yield: 2 piecrusts

1 1/2 cups flour
1 stick cold butter, sliced thick
1 teaspoon salt
5 tablespoons ice water

Place flour, butter, and salt in food processor; pulse until butter is coarsely blended. Add ice water and mix until pastry begins to form a ball. Roll out on floured surface.

✎ **Pantry checklist:** flour, butter, salt

Cream Cheese Pastry

Yield: 1 piecrust

1 cup flour
1/4 cup powdered sugar
1/8 teaspoon salt
1/2 cup butter, cold and sliced
♡*4 ounces cream cheese, cold and sliced*

Blend flour, powdered sugar, and salt in food processor. Add butter and cream cheese, slowing pulsing to form a ball. Wrap dough in plastic wrap and chill in refrigerator at least 30 minutes. When ready to use, roll dough to 10-inch round on lightly floured surface.

✎ **Grocery list:** powdered sugar, cream cheese
✎ **Pantry checklist:** flour, salt, butter

Cold-Oven Pound Cake

Yield: 18–20 servings

2 sticks butter
1/2 cup shortening
3 cups sugar
5 eggs
3 cups flour
1/8 teaspoon salt
1 teaspoon baking powder
♡*1 cup milk*
1 teaspoon vanilla

Do not preheat oven.

Cream butter, shortening, and sugar together until well blended. Add eggs 1 at a time and beat until fluffy. In a separate bowl, mix flour, salt, and baking powder together and add alternately with milk to sugar mixture. Add vanilla and beat well. Pour into well-greased and floured Bundt pan and bake in 325-degree oven 1 hour and 15 minutes (or longer) until inserted toothpick comes out clean. Start with cold oven and do not open while baking.

✎ **Pantry checklist:** butter, shortening, sugar, eggs, flour, salt, baking powder, milk, vanilla

Fudge Cupcakes with Cream Cheese Filling

Yield: 24 cupcakes

1 package super moist devil's food cake mix
1 1/3 cups water
1/2 cup vegetable oil
3 eggs

Cream Cheese Filling

♡4 ounces cream cheese, room temperature
1/3 cup sugar
1/8 teaspoon salt
1 egg
1 teaspoon vanilla

Preheat oven to 350 degrees.

Prepare cake mix as directed. Fill greased muffin tins 1/2 to 2/3 full of cake batter.

Combine filling ingredients and beat until smooth. Drop a heaping teaspoon of cream cheese filling into each cupcake and bake 15–20 minutes or until done. Frost with Creamy Chocolate Frosting on page 171.

✎ **Grocery list:** super moist devil's food cake mix, cream cheese
✎ **Pantry checklist:** vegetable oil, eggs, sugar, salt, vanilla

Coconut Cake

Yield: 15–16 slices

1 box super moist white cake mix
1 1/4 cup water
1/3 cup vegetable oil
3 egg whites
♡1 (16-ounce) container frozen whipped topping, thawed
2 cups coconut

Preheat oven to 350 degrees.

Prepare cake mix as directed. Bake in 3 (8-inch) greased and floured round cake pans for 15–18 minutes or until done. Cool on wire rack.

Frost cake with whipped topping and sprinkled with coconut. Refrigerate.

✎ **Grocery list:** super moist white cake mix, whipped topping, coconut
✎ **Pantry checklist:** vegetable oil, eggs

Hospitality Note: This cake freezes well.

Blueberry Pound Cake

Yield: 16 servings

2 cups fresh blueberries
3 cups flour, divided
2 cups sugar
1/2 cup butter, room temperature
♡*4 ounces cream cheese, room temperature*
4 large eggs
♡*1/2 cup sour cream*
2 teaspoons vanilla
2 tablespoons fresh lemon juice
2 teaspoons baking powder
1/2 teaspoon baking soda
1/2 teaspoon salt
♡*1 (6-ounce) container plain yogurt*

Preheat oven to 350 degrees.

Mix blueberries with 2 tablespoons flour (tossing to coat) and set aside. Beat sugar, butter, and cream cheese together in a large mixer bowl until well blended. Add eggs, 1 at a time, until mixed well. Then add sour cream, vanilla, and lemon juice. In a small bowl, combine remaining flour, baking powder, baking soda, and salt, mixing well. Gradually add flour mixture alternately with yogurt to egg mixture.

Remove from mixer and fold in blueberries. Pour into well-greased and floured tube pan and bake for 60–75 minutes or until done (test with toothpick after 60 minutes). Cool for 10 minutes and then remove cake to wire rack.

Glaze

1 cup powdered sugar
6–9 tablespoons fresh lemon juice

Mix powdered sugar with lemon juice. Puncture cake with fork and drizzle with glaze.

✎ **Grocery list:** blueberries, cream cheese, sour cream, lemons, yogurt, powdered sugar

✎ **Pantry checklist:** flour, sugar, butter, eggs, vanilla, baking powder, baking soda, salt

Hospitality Note: This cake will make 7 miniature loaves—great for gifts!

BUTTER-PECAN TOFFEE CAKE

Yield: 16 servings

1 box butter-pecan cake mix with pudding
4 large eggs
♡*1 cup sour cream*
1/2 cup vegetable oil
1/4 teaspoon almond extract
1 (10-ounce) package almond toffee bits
1/2 cup sweetened coconut

Preheat oven to 350 degrees.

Beat first 5 ingredients with mixer for 2 minutes or until blended. Fold in toffee bits and coconut. Spoon batter into a greased and floured tube pan. Bake 40–45 minutes or until done (test with toothpick). Cool cake on wire rack for 10 minutes.

Frosting

1/2 cup butter, melted
1 cup brown sugar
♡*1/4 cup half-and-half*
2 1/2 cups powdered sugar
1 teaspoon vanilla
1/2 cup chopped pecans or almonds

Melt butter in a small saucepan. Add brown sugar and cook until sugar is dissolved, stirring occasionally. Remove from heat and stir in half-and-half, powdered sugar, and vanilla. Beat with mixer until smooth and creamy. Frost cake and sprinkle with pecans or almonds.

✎ **Grocery list:** butter-pecan cake mix with pudding, sour cream, almond toffee bits, coconut, half-and-half, powdered sugar, pecans or almonds

✎ **Pantry checklist:** eggs, vegetable oil, almond extract, butter, brown sugar, vanilla

Tiramisu Toffee Torte

Yield: 14–16 servings

1 white cake mix with pudding
1 cup strong coffee, room temperature
4 egg whites
6 ounces chocolate-covered toffee bits, divided

Preheat oven to 350 degrees.

Grease and flour 3 (8-inch) round cake pans. In a large bowl, combine cake mix, coffee, and egg whites. Beat at low speed until moistened; beat 2 minutes at high speed. Fold in 4 ounces toffee bits. Spread in pans and bake 15–20 minutes or until inserted toothpick comes out clean. Cool 10 minutes. Remove from pans and cool completely.

Frosting

2/3 cup sugar
1/3 cup chocolate syrup
♡*4 ounces cream cheese, room temperature*
♡*2 cups whipping cream or whipped topping*
2 teaspoons vanilla
1 cup strong coffee, room temperature

Combine sugar, chocolate syrup, and cream cheese and beat until smooth. Add whipping cream or whipped topping and vanilla. Beat until light and fluffy. Refrigerate until ready to use.

To assemble cake, drizzle each layer with 1/3 cup coffee. Place layer—coffee side up—on serving plate; spread with frosting. Repeat with second and third layers. Frost sides and top of cake with remaining frosting and garnish with 2 ounces toffee bits. Store in refrigerator.

✎ **Grocery list:** white cake mix with pudding, chocolate-covered toffee bits, chocolate syrup, cream cheese, whipping cream or whipped topping

✎ **Pantry checklist:** coffee, eggs, sugar, vanilla

Hospitality Note: I always bake the cake layers in advance and freeze them. I also frost them while they are frozen, which makes the icing much easier to spread.

CARROT CAKE WITH CREAM CHEESE FROSTING

Yield: 15–16 servings

2 cups flour
2 teaspoons baking soda
1/2 teaspoon salt
2 teaspoons cinnamon
3 large eggs
2 cups sugar
3/4 cup vegetable oil
♡*3/4 cup buttermilk*
2 teaspoons vanilla
2 cups grated carrot
1 (8-ounce) can crushed pineapple, drained
1 (3 1/2-ounce) can flaked coconut
1 cup chopped pecans

Preheat oven to 350 degrees.

Blend first 4 ingredients and set aside. With the mixer, beat eggs and next 4 ingredients together at medium speed until smooth. Add flour mixture, beating at low speed until blended. Fold in carrots, crushed pineapple, coconut, and pecans. Pour into 3 (8-inch) greased and floured round cake pans and bake 25–30 minutes or until done. Cool on wire rack.

Cream Cheese Frosting

♡*1 (8-ounce) package cream cheese, room temperature*
1/4 cup butter, softened
♡*2–3 tablespoons milk*
1 teaspoon vanilla
1 (1-pound) box powdered sugar

Beat cream cheese, butter, milk, and vanilla in a medium bowl with electric mixer on slow speed until smooth. Gradually beat in powdered sugar, 1 cup at a time, on low speed until the frosting is smooth and easy to spread. Frost between and on top and sides of cooled cake layers.

✎ **Grocery list:** buttermilk, carrots, crushed pineapple, coconut, pecans, cream cheese, powdered sugar

✎ **Pantry checklist:** flour, baking soda, salt, cinnamon, eggs, sugar, vegetable oil, vanilla, butter, milk

Chocolate Fudge Cake

Yield: 15 servings

1 box chocolate fudge cake mix
1 package (3.4 ounces) instant chocolate pudding
♡*1 cup milk*
♡*1/2 cup sour cream*
4 eggs

Preheat oven to 350 degrees.

Combine all ingredients in a large mixer bowl. Beat on low speed just until blended. Beat on high speed for 2 minutes. Pour into greased and floured Bundt pan and bake 55–65 minutes or until a toothpick inserted in the cake comes out clean. Cool in pan for 20 minutes.

Glaze

2 ounces semisweet baking chocolate, melted
1 1/2 cups powdered sugar
3 tablespoons butter, melted
1 teaspoon vanilla

Mix together and drizzle over cake.

✎ **Grocery list:** chocolate fudge cake mix, instant chocolate pudding, sour cream, semisweet baking chocolate, powdered sugar

✎ **Pantry checklist:** milk, eggs, butter, vanilla

Note: I've found that melting chocolate on the defrost setting of the microwave is the best way to keep it from burning.

Chocolate Toffee Cake

Yield: 15–16 servings

1 box chocolate fudge cake mix
1 1/3 cups water
1/2 cup vegetable oil
3 eggs

Preheat oven to 350 degrees.

Prepare cake mix as directed. Pour into 3 (8-inch) greased and floured round cake pans.

Bake 15–17 minutes or until done. Cool in pans for 5 minutes. Then remove to a wire rack to continue cooling.

Frosting

♡*1 (8-ounce) package cream cheese, room temperature*
1 cup powdered sugar
1/2 cup granulated sugar
1 (8-ounce) package chocolate-covered toffee bits
♡*1 (12-ounce) container frozen whipped topping, thawed*

Beat cream cheese, powdered sugar, and granulated sugar with mixer until frosting is creamy. Add toffee bits and whipped topping.

Frost cake and keep in refrigerator.

✎ **Grocery list:** chocolate fudge cake mix, cream cheese, powdered sugar, chocolate-covered toffee bits, whipped topping

✎ **Pantry checklist:** vegetable oil, eggs, granulated sugar

Hospitality Note: This cake freezes well.

German-Chocolate Pecan Cake

Yield: 15–16 servings

1 box German chocolate cake mix
1 1/3 cups water
1/2 cup vegetable oil
3 eggs

Preheat oven to 350 degrees.

Prepare cake mix as directed. Pour into 3 (8-inch) well-greased and floured cake pans and bake 15–18 minutes or until done. Cool on wire rack.

Frosting

1 (15-ounce) can coconut-pecan frosting
♡1 (16-ounce) container frozen whipped topping, thawed
1 (3.4-ounce) instant chocolate pudding

Mix coconut-pecan frosting, whipped topping, and instant pudding in mixer until well blended. Frost between the layers and on top and sides of the cake. Store in refrigerator.

✎ **Grocery list:** German-chocolate cake mix, coconut-pecan frosting, whipped topping, instant chocolate pudding

✎ **Pantry checklist:** vegetable oil, eggs

Hospitality Note: This can be prepared ahead of time and frozen.

PUMPKIN-PECAN CAKE WITH PRALINE SAUCE

Yield: 16 servings

3/4 cup chopped pecans
3 cups flour
2 tablespoons pumpkin pie spice
2 teaspoons baking soda
1 teaspoon salt
1 cup butter, softened
1 cup brown sugar
1 cup granulated sugar
4 large eggs
1 (15-ounce) can pumpkin
1 teaspoon vanilla

Preheat oven to 350 degrees.

Grease a tube pan and sprinkle pecans on the bottom of the pan. Combine flour, pumpkin pie spice, baking soda, and salt and set aside. Cream butter with brown sugar and granulated sugar in mixer until well blended. Add eggs, 1 at a time, and blend well. Add pumpkin and vanilla and beat well. Gradually add flour mixture to the butter-eggs mixture, mixing well. Spoon batter into the greased and floured pan and bake for 60 minutes or until inserted toothpick comes out clean. Cool 10 minutes.

Praline Sauce

♡1 cup corn syrup
1/2 cup sugar
1/3 cup butter
1 egg, lightly beaten
1 cup chopped pecans
1 teaspoon vanilla

Mix corn syrup, sugar, butter, and egg in a saucepan. Bring to boil over medium heat, stirring constantly. Boil for 2 minutes. Remove from heat and stir in pecans and vanilla. Make holes in cake with fork and pour icing on top.

✎ **Grocery list:** pecans, pumpkin

✎ **Pantry checklist:** flour, pumpkin pie spice, baking soda, salt, butter, brown sugar, granulated sugar, eggs, vanilla, corn syrup

Pineapple Upside-Down Cake

Yield: 15–16 servings

1/4 cup butter
1 cup brown sugar
1 (20-ounce) can pineapple slices, drained and juice reserved
1 (6-ounce) jar maraschino cherries, drained
1 package super moist yellow cake mix
1/3 cup vegetable oil
3 eggs
♡whipped topping, to serve

Preheat oven to 350 degrees.

Melt butter in 9-x-13-inch baking dish in oven. Sprinkle brown sugar evenly over butter. Arrange pineapple slices over brown sugar. Place cherry in center of each pineapple ring and around edges of pan.

Add enough water to pineapple juice to make 1 1/4 cups. Beat cake mix, pineapple juice mixture, oil, and eggs in mixer on low for 30 seconds, then on medium speed for 2 minutes. Pour cake mixture over pineapple and bake 40–45 minutes or until inserted toothpick comes out clean.

Run knife around edge of pan. Turn cake upside down onto heatproof dish and leave pan on top for 1–2 minutes so topping can drizzle over cake. Cool 30 minutes. Serve with whipped topping.

✎ **Grocery list:** pineapple slices, maraschino cherries, super moist yellow cake mix, whipped topping

✎ **Pantry checklist:** butter, brown sugar, vegetable oil, eggs

Brown Sugar and Pineapple Cake

Yield: 15–16 servings

1 package super moist yellow cake mix
4 eggs
♡*1 cup sour cream*
1 cup vegetable oil
1/4 cup water

Preheat oven to 325 degrees.

Combine cake mix with the other ingredients. Beat in the mixer for 2–3 minutes or until well blended.

Filling

1/3 cup butter
3/4 cup brown sugar
1 (20-ounce) can crushed pineapple, drained
1/2 cup chopped pecans

While mixing cake, melt butter and brown sugar in saucepan and cook until well blended. Stir in pineapple and pecans. Pour one half of pineapple mixture in bottom of well-greased and floured Bundt pan; spoon one half of cake mix mixture on top of pineapple mixture and repeat layers. Bake 60 minutes or until inserted toothpick comes out clean. Cool in pan 10–12 minutes before removing to cake plate.

✎ **Grocery list:** super moist yellow cake mix with pudding, sour cream, crushed pineapple, pecans

✎ **Pantry checklist:** eggs, vegetable oil, butter, brown sugar

Pineapple Cake

Yield: 15–16 servings

1 box super moist white cake mix
$1\frac{1}{4}$ cups water
$\frac{1}{3}$ cup vegetable oil
3 egg whites

Preheat oven to 350 degrees.

Prepare cake mix as directed. Bake in 3 (8-inch) greased and floured round cake pans 15–18 minutes or until done. Cool on wire rack.

Filling

4 tablespoons flour
$\frac{1}{2}$ cup sugar
1 (20-ounce) can crushed pineapple, undrained
2 tablespoons butter

Combine flour and sugar in a medium saucepan. Add crushed pineapple and butter and cook until thickened.

Cream Cheese Frosting

♡1 (8-ounce) package cream cheese, room temperature
$\frac{1}{4}$ cup butter, softened
♡2–3 tablespoons milk
1 teaspoon vanilla
1 (1-pound) box powdered sugar

Beat cream cheese, butter, milk, and vanilla in a medium bowl with electric mixer on slow speed until smooth. Gradually beat in powdered sugar, 1 cup at a time, on low speed until the frosting is smooth and easy to spread.

To assemble cake, spread filling between layers. Then frost top and sides of cake with cream cheese frosting.

✎ **Grocery list:** super moist white cake mix, crushed pineapple, cream cheese, powdered sugar

✎ **Pantry checklist:** vegetable oil, eggs, flour, sugar, butter, milk, vanilla

CHOCOLATE TURTLE CAKE

Yield: 15 servings

1 package super moist devil's food cake mix
1 1/3 cups water
1/2 cup vegetable oil
3 eggs
1 (16-ounce) jar caramel topping
♡*1/2 cup evaporated milk*
3/4 cup chocolate-covered toffee bits
3/4 cup chopped pecans, toasted
♡*vanilla ice cream and fudge sauce, to serve*

Preheat oven to 350 degrees.

Combine first 4 ingredients and mix according to directions on box. Pour half of batter into a greased 9-x-13-inch pan and bake 15–20 minutes or until done. While cake is baking, heat caramel syrup and milk, mixing well. When cake is finished, punch holes in it with a fork and pour caramel mixture over warm cake. Sprinkle with toffee bits and pecans. Pour remaining cake mixture on top and bake another 20–25 minutes. Serve warm with vanilla ice cream and fudge sauce.

✎ **Grocery list:** super moist devil's food cake mix, caramel topping, evaporated milk, chocolate-covered toffee bits, pecans, ice cream, fudge sauce

✎ **Pantry checklist:** vegetable oil, eggs

Oreo Cake

Yield: 15–16 servings

1 package super moist devil's food cake mix
1 1/3 cups water
1/2 cup vegetable oil
3 eggs

Preheat oven to 350 degrees.

Mix cake according to directions. Spread mix in 3 (8-inch) greased and floured round cake pans. Bake 15–18 minutes or until done. Cool on wire rack.

Frosting

♡4 ounces cream cheese, room temperature
3/4 cup powdered sugar
♡1 (16-ounce) container frozen whipped topping, thawed
♡10 Oreo cookies, crushed
miniature Oreo cookies to garnish

Thoroughly mix cream cheese, powdered sugar, and whipped topping. Fold crushed Oreos into mixture. Frost between and on top and sides of cake layers. Store in refrigerator. Garnish with miniature Oreo cookies.

✎ **Grocery list:** super moist devil's food cake mix, cream cheese, powdered sugar, whipped topping, Oreo cookies, miniature Oreo cookies

✎ **Pantry checklist:** vegetable oil, eggs

CHOCOLATE ESPRESSO CAKE

Yield: 15–16 servings

1 tablespoon instant coffee or espresso (dry)
1⅓ cups water
1 package super moist German chocolate cake mix
½ cup vegetable oil
3 eggs

Preheat oven to 350 degrees.

Combine instant coffee and water and add cake mix, oil, and eggs. Beat in mixer according to directions for cake. Spoon into 3 (8-inch) greased and floured round cake pans. Bake 15–20 minutes or until done. Cool on wire rack.

Frosting

2 teaspoons instant coffee or espresso (dry)
1 tablespoon cool water
1 (12-ounce) container cream cheese frosting
♡ *1½ cups frozen whipped topping, thawed*

Dissolve coffee in water and mix with cream cheese frosting and whipped topping. Frost between and on top and sides of layers. Store in refrigerator.

✎ **Grocery list:** instant coffee, super moist German chocolate cake mix, cream cheese frosting , whipped topping
✎ **Pantry checklist:** vegetable oil, eggs

Chocolate Italian Cream Cake

Yield: 15–16 servings

1 box super moist chocolate fudge cake mix
1 1/3 cups water
1/2 cup vegetable oil
3 eggs
3/4 cup coconut
1/2 cup chopped pecans

Preheat oven to 350 degrees.

Prepare cake mix as directed and add coconut and pecans. Spoon batter into 3 (8-inch) well-greased and floured round cake pans and bake 15–18 minutes or until done.

Cream Cheese Frosting

♡1 (8-ounce) package cream cheese, room temperature
1/4 cup butter, softened
♡2–3 tablespoons milk
1 teaspoon vanilla
1 (1-pound) box powdered sugar

Beat cream cheese, butter, milk, and vanilla in a medium bowl with electric mixer on slow speed until smooth. Gradually beat in powdered sugar, 1 cup at a time, on low speed until the frosting is smooth and easy to spread. Frost between and on top and sides of cooled cake layers.

✎ **Grocery list:** super moist chocolate fudge cake mix, coconut, pecans, cream cheese, powdered sugar

✎ **Pantry checklist:** vegetable oil, eggs, butter, milk, vanilla

BROWNIE-TOFFEE TRIFLE

Yield: 8–10 servings

1 package fudge brownie mix or chocolate cake mix (Note the ingredients required to prepare the mix.)
1 (8-ounce) package chocolate-covered toffee bits
♡1 (16-ounce) container frozen whipped topping, thawed, divided

Chocolate Pudding

1 cup sugar
1/8 teaspoon salt
1/4 cup cocoa
4 1/2 tablespoons cornstarch
3 egg yolks
♡2 1/2 cups milk
1/4 teaspoon almond flavoring
1 tablespoon butter

Preheat oven to 350 degrees.

Bake brownies or cake mix according to box instructions. Cool and break into small pieces.

Mix sugar, salt, cocoa, and cornstarch in a medium saucepan. Mix egg yolks and milk together with whisk and add to sugar mixture. Cook over medium heat until thickened. Remove from heat and add almond flavoring and butter; cool. Add 8 ounces whipped topping to chocolate pudding.

In trifle dish, layer brownies or cake, pudding mixture, 8 ounces of whipped topping, and toffee bits. Repeat layers and refrigerate. Cover and chill for several hours.

✎ **Grocery list:** fudge brownie mix or chocolate cake mix, chocolate-covered toffee bits, whipped topping

✎ **Pantry checklist:** sugar, salt, cocoa, cornstarch, eggs, milk, almond flavoring, butter

> ***Hospitality Note:*** Keep baked brownies in your freezer for this dish or just a quick dessert.

Easy Caramel Frosting

Yield: frosting for 2-layer (9-inch) cake

1/2 cup butter

1 cup brown sugar

♡*1/4 cup half-and-half (I use fat-free half-and-half in this recipe.)*

2 1/2 cups powdered sugar

1 teaspoon vanilla

Melt butter in a medium saucepan. Add brown sugar and cook until sugar is dissolved, stirring occasionally. Stir in half-and-half. Add powdered sugar and vanilla. Beat in mixer until smooth and creamy.

✎ **Grocery list:** half-and-half, powdered sugar

✎ **Pantry checklist:** butter, brown sugar, vanilla

Cream Cheese Frosting

Yield: frosting for 1 cake

♡*1 (8-ounce) package cream cheese, room temperature*

1/4 cup butter, softened

♡*2–3 tablespoons milk*

1 teaspoon vanilla

1 (1-pound) box powdered sugar

Beat cream cheese, butter, milk, and vanilla in a medium bowl with electric mixer on slow speed until smooth. Gradually beat in powdered sugar, 1 cup at a time, on low speed until frosting is smooth and spreadable.

✎ **Grocery list:** cream cheese, powdered sugar

✎ **Pantry checklist:** butter, milk, vanilla

Creamy White Frosting

Yield: frosting for 1 cake

♡½ *cup shortening*
♡4 *ounces cream cheese, room temperature*
¼ *cup marshmallow cream*
1 *teaspoon vanilla*
⅛ *teaspoon almond flavoring*
1 *(1-pound) box powdered sugar*
♡2–3 *tablespoons milk, depending on desired consistency*

Cream shortening with cream cheese. Add remaining ingredients. Beat with mixer until consistency is smooth and easy to spread.

✎ **Grocery list:** cream cheese, marshmallow cream, powdered sugar
✎ **Pantry checklist:** shortening, vanilla, almond flavoring, milk

> ***Hospitality Note:*** Keep this frosting in refrigerator for occasions when you need to save time.

Creamy Chocolate Frosting

Yield: frosting for 1 cake

1 *(1-pound) box powdered sugar*
1 *stick butter, softened*
1 *teaspoon vanilla*
3 *ounces semisweet baking chocolate, melted*
♡¼ *cup milk (or more, depending on desired consistency)*

Mix powdered sugar and butter in the mixer on low speed. Stir in vanilla and chocolate. Gradually beat in just enough milk to make the frosting spreadable.

✎ **Grocery list:** powdered sugar, semisweet baking chocolate
✎ **Pantry checklist:** butter, vanilla, milk

Chocolate Chip Cookies

Yield: about 2 dozen cookies

1/2 cup butter, softened
1/2 cup brown sugar
1/4 cup granulated sugar
1 large egg
1 teaspoon vanilla
1 1/4 cups flour
1/2 teaspoon baking soda
1/2 teaspoon salt
3/4 cup semisweet miniature chocolate chips
1/4 cup chocolate-covered toffee bits
1/2 cup pecan pieces

Preheat oven to 375 degrees.

In a large bowl, mix butter with brown sugar and granulated sugar until creamy. Beat in egg and vanilla. Reduce speed to low and mix in flour, baking soda, and salt until blended. Stir in chocolate chips, toffee bits, and pecans.

Drop by teaspoons onto nonstick cookie sheet and bake 9–10 minutes or until browned.

✎ **Grocery list:** semisweet miniature chocolate chips, chocolate-covered toffee bits, pecans

✎ **Pantry checklist:** butter, brown sugar, granulated sugar, egg, vanilla, flour, baking soda, salt

CHRISTMAS BUTTER COOKIES

Yield: 50 cookies

1 cup butter, softened
1 cup sugar
1 large egg
1 teaspoon vanilla
3 cups flour
2 teaspoons baking powder
powdered sugar

Preheat oven to 350 degrees.

Cream butter and sugar in mixer until creamy. Mix in egg and vanilla. Add flour and baking powder and mix well. Roll out cookies on surface sprinkled with powdered sugar. Cut with cookie cutters or use cookie press. Bake 8–10 minutes or until lightly browned.

Frosting

3 cups powdered sugar
1 teaspoon vanilla
♡*2–4 tablespoons milk (or more, depending on desired consistency)*

Mix together sugar, vanilla, and enough milk to make spreading or drizzling consistency.

✎ **Grocery list:** powdered sugar
✎ **Pantry checklist:** butter, sugar, egg, vanilla, flour, baking powder, milk

Note: Gather your grandchildren or neighborhood kids and all the colored sugar crystals you can find. Then let the little ones be creative with the cookies!

Hospitality Note: These cookies freeze well.

Apricot Cookies

Yield: 4 dozen cookies

1 cup butter, softened
1 cup granulated sugar
1 egg yolk
2 cups flour
1 teaspoon grated orange peel
powdered sugar
1/3 cup apricot preserves

Preheat oven to 350 degrees.

In a large mixing bowl, beat butter with electric mixer on medium to high speed for 30 seconds. Add sugar and blend until well mixed, scraping sides of bowl occasionally. Add egg yolk. Gradually add flour and orange peel.

On surface sprinkled with powdered sugar, roll cookie dough to 1/2 inch. Using 1 1/2-inch round cookie cutter, cut into rounds. Press your thumb into the center and fill each indent with 1/4 teaspoon apricot preserves.

Bake 10–12 minutes until edges are lightly browned. Cool.

Glaze

1 tablespoon shortening
6 ounces semisweet baking chocolate

Melt shortening and chocolate together. Dip half of cookie in chocolate mixture. Place on wire rack to set.

✎ **Grocery list:** orange, powdered sugar, apricot preserves, semisweet baking chocolate

✎ **Pantry checklist:** butter, sugar, egg, flour, shortening

Hospitality Note: These cookies freeze well.

RASPBERRY COOKIES

Yield: 3½ dozen cookies

⅔ cup sugar
1 cup butter, softened
½ teaspoon vanilla
2 cups flour
½ cup raspberry preserves

Preheat oven to 350 degrees.

Combine sugar, butter, and vanilla. Beat in mixer on medium speed until creamy. Reduce speed to low and gradually add flour. Mix well. Cover dough and chill 1 hour. Shape dough into 1-inch balls. Place 2 inches apart on nonstick cookie sheet. With thumb, make indentation in center of each cookie and fill each indent with ¼ teaspoon raspberry preserves. Bake 10–12 minutes or until lightly browned. Let set 1 minute. Then remove from cookie sheet.

Glaze

1 cup powdered sugar
1 teaspoon vanilla
2–3 teaspoons water

Combine powdered sugar, vanilla, and water to make a thin icing. Drizzle icing on cooled cookies.

✎ **Grocery list:** raspberry preserves, powdered sugar

✎ **Pantry checklist:** sugar, butter, vanilla, flour

Hospitality Note: These cookies freeze well.

Spiced Almond Bars

Yield: 32 bars

2 sticks butter, softened
1 cup sugar
1 teaspoon cinnamon
1 teaspoon nutmeg
1 egg, separated
2 cups flour
1 3/4 cups sliced almonds

Preheat oven to 300 degrees.

Cream butter in a large mixer. Add sugar, cinnamon, and nutmeg, mixing well. Add egg yolk and blend. Gradually add the 2 cups of flour; dough will be stiff.

Line a 10-x-15-inch baking pan with foil; rub with butter. Place dough in pan and press to edges. (Cover dough with plastic wrap. Press to smooth it evenly in pan.) Beat egg white until foamy, then brush over dough. Sprinkle almonds evenly over top. Use plastic wrap again and lightly press almonds into dough with fingers. Bake 40–45 minutes.

Glaze

1 cup powdered sugar
1 tablespoon butter, melted
1 tablespoon water
1 tablespoon lemon juice

Mix glaze ingredients together and pour over baked cake. Cool for 15 minutes. Lift cake and foil out of pan and slide cake onto cutting board and cut into squares.

✎ **Grocery list:** almonds, powdered sugar
✎ **Pantry checklist:** butter, sugar, cinnamon, nutmeg, egg, flour, lemon juice

LIME BARS

Yield: 30 bars

2 1/2 cups flour, divided
1/2 cup powdered sugar
3/4 cup butter
1/2 teaspoon baking powder
4 large eggs, lightly beaten
2 cups granulated sugar
1/2 teaspoon grated lime rind
1/3 cup lime juice
1 drop green food coloring
sifted powdered sugar
fresh strawberries, for garnish

Preheat oven to 350 degrees.

Combine 2 cups flour and 1/2 powdered sugar. Cut in butter with pastry blender or food processor. Firmly press mixture into a lightly greased 9-x-13-inch dish and bake for 20–25 minutes or until lightly browned.

Combine remaining 1/2 cup flour and baking powder in a small bowl and stir well. In a large bowl, mix eggs, sugar, lime rind, and lime juice. Stir in flour mixture. Add food coloring, mix, and pour over prepared crust. Bake 25 minutes or until set. After completely cool, sprinkle with sifted powdered sugar. Cut in squares and serve with a fresh strawberry on top for garnish.

✎ **Grocery list:** powdered sugar, limes, fresh strawberries

✎ **Pantry checklist:** flour, butter, baking powder, eggs, sugar, green food coloring

MINIATURE CREAM PUFFS

Yield: 50 small puffs

1/2 cup butter
1 cup boiling water
1 cup flour
1/4 teaspoon salt
4 eggs

Preheat oven to 400 degrees.

Melt butter in boiling water. Add flour and salt, stirring vigorously until mixture forms a ball. Remove from heat and cool slightly. Add eggs, 1 at a time, mixing well after each addition until eggs are absorbed.

Using teaspoon, form pastry into small balls and place on nonstick ungreased baking sheet. Bake 10 minutes, then reduce temperature to 325 degrees and bake 15–20 minutes more or until pastries have browned. Cool on wire rack.

Filling

1 cup sugar
4 1/2 tablespoons cornstarch
dash of salt
3 egg yolks
♡2 1/2 cups milk
2 tablespoons butter
1 teaspoon vanilla

Mix sugar, cornstarch, and salt in a medium saucepan and set aside. With whisk blend egg yolks and milk and add to sugar mixture. Cook on medium heat until mixture thickens. Remove from heat and add butter and vanilla. Refrigerate pudding to cool.

To assemble puffs, cut top from puff and fill with pudding. Place top back on cream puff and drizzle with chocolate glaze.

Chocolate Glaze

3 (1-ounce) squares of semisweet baking chocolate
♡3 teaspoons milk
1 cup powdered sugar (more or less, depending on desired consistency)

Melt chocolate and add milk. Mix in powdered sugar with a wire whisk.

✎ **Grocery list:** semisweet baking chocolate, powdered sugar
✎ **Pantry checklist:** butter, flour, salt, eggs, sugar, cornstarch, milk, vanilla

> ***Hospitality Note:*** Puffs can be made in advance (up to a week) and kept in a closed container in cool area. Fill just prior to serving.

EASY APPLE TURNOVERS

Yield: 6–8 servings

Delicious and quick!

6 apples, peeled and thinly sliced
1/4 cup sugar (or more) or sweetener
1 tablespoon butter
1/8 teaspoon cinnamon
1/8 teaspoon nutmeg
6–8 (8-inch) flour tortillas
♡ice cream, caramel syrup, pecans, to serve

In saucepan, cook apples over low to medium heat until done. Add sugar or sweetener, butter, cinnamon, and nutmeg and stir well. Place equal portions of apple mixture in center of tortillas and fold over. Spray skillet with nonstick cooking spray. Brown tortillas. When serving, drizzle with caramel syrup and sprinkle with chopped pecans.

✎ **Grocery list:** apples, flour tortillas, ice cream, caramel syrup, pecans
✎ **Pantry checklist:** sugar, butter, cinnamon, nutmeg

SALTINE CRACKER CANDY

Yield: 12 or more servings

♡31 saltine crackers
1 cup butter
1 cup brown sugar
1 (12-ounce) bag chocolate chips

Preheat oven to 400 degrees.

Cover 9-x-13-inch cookie sheet with aluminum foil and fill with saltine crackers. Melt butter and brown sugar and boil about 5 minutes. Pour over crackers and bake 5 minutes. Remove from oven and sprinkle chocolate chips on top. Cool for a few minutes, then place in refrigerator until hard. Break into pieces and enjoy!

✎ **Grocery list:** saltine crackers, chocolate chips
✎ **Pantry checklist:** butter, brown sugar

Hot Fudge Sauce

Yield: 3 cups

1 (16-ounce) can chocolate syrup
1 stick butter
1 teaspoon vanilla
1/4 teaspoon salt
♡*1 can sweetened condensed milk*

Heat chocolate syrup and butter in heavy saucepan over medium heat just until boiling. Add vanilla, salt, and condensed milk, stirring constantly. Reduce heat and continue to stir until well mixed. Keep on low temperature for several minutes until mixture gets thick and creamy. Remove from heat.

✎ **Grocery list:** chocolate syrup, condensed milk

✎ **Pantry checklist:** butter, vanilla, salt

Hospitality Note: Drizzle over an ice cream sundae, ice cream pie, or chocolate cake. This keeps well in the refrigerator and makes a great gift.

Closing Thoughts

During our forty-seven years of marriage, Jack and I have been privileged to welcome many people into our home. It has also been a joy to be the recipient of wonderful hospitality in the home of friends and family, which now includes our four married children, who are the parents of our fifteen grandchildren.

For the first twelve years of our married life, Jack played professional football, so we lived in the five cities where he played. Most of the players went back home only for the off-season, which meant that the players and their families were family to each other for the six-month football season. We celebrated holidays and our children's birthdays together. To this day, some of my favorite recipes are from players' wives, who hailed from all parts of the country. We Californians were introduced to grits, southern ham, and black-eyed peas! One friend had never eaten lamb until I disguised it (marinated, butterflied, and grilled). To his surprise, he liked it!

When Jack was elected to Congress in 1970, we moved from Buffalo, New York, to Bethesda, Maryland, which has been our home now for thirty-five years. It was here that our children spent most of their growing-up years. Since Congress met into the evening, our dinnertime fell between 8:00 and 8:30 p.m. so Jack could be there. I allowed the children to eat healthy snacks around 6:00 p.m. The opportunities for family dinners pass by quickly, and we are grateful we made them a priority until our youngest child left for college. Our meal pattern was set—the two of us *still* prefer dinner at home around 8:00 p.m.

Jack has brought interesting people home for dinner frequently over the past thirty-five years. When our children were living with us, they helped serve and clean up, and of course they always ate with us. They were exposed to wonderful discussions with fascinating guests such as Ambassador Jeane Kirkpatrick and her late husband, Kirk; former prime minister of Israel Benjamin Netanyahu; the late Bob Hope; numerous senators and congressmen; the late astronaut Alan Shepard Jr. and his late wife, Louise; and the late Dr. Francis Schaeffer and his wife, Edith. Many of our friends still express pleasure at the way Jimmy, our youngest son, would say good night by name to each person around the table.

Our oval dining room table seats up to twelve people comfortably, and this encourages in-depth discussions from a sizable group. Either Jack or I will throw out a question to help us learn something about each other, such as "How much of your childhood was spent in one place? Why and what did you learn there?" or "Which current or historical leader do you most admire?"

For over thirty years our home has been the setting for a weekly women's discussion and prayer time that often includes lunch. The food served is less important than the relationships that have developed in our safe support group—a group that enjoys discussing the moral issues of our culture from both secular and biblical world-view perspectives.

Edith Schaeffer, who has authored many books and is now in her nineties, inspired me to focus on people and use my God-given creativity to provide a pleasant and relaxed environment for meals and substantive conversations. Over the years I've become less concerned about details and found flexibility to be essential. Many providential opportunities for hospitality would be missed if we waited for the perfect time to invite guests into our home. A relaxed and welcoming spirit covers over most imperfections.

I've found it helpful to pray that guests in our home are the people of God's choice and that our conversation edifies and glorifies God and His creation. We want to put our guests at ease. We also want to provide food, fun, comfort, counsel, help, and companionship in each gathering of unique people.

As we live our earthly lives, I'm grateful for the opportunities we have had to gather around tables in homes for meals and to experience the pleasure of companionship with fellow pilgrims. May the joy of knowing our Savior, Christ Jesus, be an increasing part of our walk here on earth and into eternity. Since God created us for fellowship with Him and each other, may our homes be a welcoming haven.

—Joanne Kemp
wife of former senator and presidential
candidate Jack Kemp

Favorite Substitutions

Use this helpful guide when you need to substitute ingredients in a recipe. (This list is adapted from www.landolakes.com/mealideas/Substitutions.cfm and is provided by www.landolakes.com and Land O'Lakes, Inc. Look there for other helpful ideas.)

Allspice, ground—1/4 teaspoon ground cinnamon plus 1/2 teaspoon ground cloves plus 1/4 teaspoon ground nutmeg can be substituted for 1 teaspoon ground allspice.

Baking powder—1/4 teaspoon baking soda plus 1/2 teaspoon cream of tartar can be substituted for 1 teaspoon baking powder.

Butter—Unsalted butter can be substituted for regular butter in any recipe. It is *not* necessary to add salt. Whipped butter can be used as a substitute for stick butter, based on weight, not volume.

Buttermilk—1 tablespoon vinegar plus enough milk to equal 1 cup ***or*** 2/3 cup plain yogurt plus 1/3 cup milk can be substituted for 1 cup buttermilk.

Chicken or beef broth—1 cup hot water plus 1 teaspoon instant bouillon granules (or 1 bouillon cube) can be substituted for 1 cup broth.

Chili sauce—1 cup tomato sauce, 1/4 cup brown sugar, 2 tablespoons vinegar, 1/4 teaspoon cinnamon, a dash of ground cloves, plus a dash of allspice can be substituted for 1 cup of chili sauce.

Chives—1 teaspoon green onion tops, finely chopped, equals 1 teaspoon chives.

Chocolate chips, semisweet—6 ounces semisweet chocolate, chopped, can be substituted for 1 cup (6 ounces) semisweet chocolate chips. When substituting for chocolate chips, make sure to use the same type of chocolate (e.g., semisweet, milk).

Chocolate, semisweet—3 tablespoons chocolate chips ***or*** 1 square (1-ounce) unsweetened chocolate plus 1 tablespoon sugar can be substituted for 1 square (1-ounce) semisweet chocolate; 6 tablespoons unsweetened cocoa powder plus 7 tablespoons sugar plus 1/4 cup butter can be substituted for 6 ounces semisweet chocolate. Bittersweet chocolate can be substituted for semisweet chocolate, although there could be a slight difference in texture and flavor.

Chocolate, sweet baking (German's)—½ cup unsweetened cocoa powder plus ⅓ cup sugar plus 3 tablespoons butter, margarine, or shortening can be substituted for 4 ounces German's sweet baking chocolate.

Chocolate, unsweetened—⅔ ounce semisweet chocolate (reduce sugar in recipe by 2 teaspoons) ***or*** 3 tablespoons unsweetened cocoa plus 1 tablespoon butter, margarine, or shortening can be substituted for 1 ounce unsweetened baking chocolate.

Cinnamon, ground—½ teaspoon ground allspice or 1 teaspoon ground cardamom can be substituted for 1 teaspoon ground cinnamon.

Cocoa, unsweetened—Dutch-processed cocoa may be substituted for unsweetened cocoa.

Coffee—½ cup hot water plus 1 teaspoon instant coffee granules can be substituted for ½ cup strong, brewed coffee.

Cooking sprays—They can usually be successfully substituted for shortening to grease baking sheets and baking pans.

Cornmeal, self-rising—⅞ cup plain cornmeal plus 1½ tablespoons baking powder plus ½ teaspoon salt can be substituted for 1 cup self-rising cornmeal.

Cornstarch—2 tablespoons all-purpose flour or 2 teaspoons arrowroot starch can be substituted for 1 tablespoon cornstarch.

Corn syrup, light—1 cup dark corn syrup can be substituted for 1 cup light corn syrup, and vice versa. (Note: Flavor will be affected somewhat.) Or substitute 1¼ cups sugar plus ⅓ cup whatever liquid is called for in the recipe.

Eggs—2 egg whites can be substituted for 1 whole egg; ¼ cup refrigerated egg substitute can be substituted for 1 egg.

Egg whites—Meringue powder can be substituted for egg whites in a meringue application only. Three tablespoons meringue powder plus 6 tablespoons water equal approximately 3 egg whites. Powdered egg whites may be substituted in most recipes requiring egg whites. Follow directions on powdered egg whites container.

Flour, all-purpose—Self-rising flour minus the salt called for in yeast-bread recipes can be substituted for all-purpose flour. Self-rising flour minus the salt and baking powder called for in quick-bread recipes can be substituted for all-purpose flour. One cup plus 2 tablespoons cake flour can be substituted for 1 cup all-purpose flour. In recipes such as quick breads and pancakes, 20 percent of all-purpose flour with another grain, such as rye, buckwheat, or soy flour, can be substituted for all-purpose flour.

Flour (as thickener)—1 tablespoon quick-cooking tapioca ***or*** 1/2 tablespoon cornstarch, potato starch, rice starch, or arrowroot starch can be substituted for 1 tablespoon all-purpose flour.

Flour, cake—1 cup minus 2 tablespoons all-purpose flour can be substituted for 1 cup cake flour.

Flour, self-rising—1 cup all-purpose flour plus 1 1/2 teaspoons baking powder plus 1/2 teaspoon salt can be substituted for 1 cup self-rising flour.

Garlic—1/8 to 1/4 teaspoon instant minced garlic or 1/8 teaspoon garlic powder can be substituted for 1 clove minced garlic.

Ginger, ground—1/2 teaspoon ground mace plus 1/2 teaspoon grated lemon peel can be substituted for 1 teaspoon ground ginger.

Honey—1 1/4 cups sugar plus 1/3 cup liquid (use whatever liquid is called for in the recipe) can be substituted for 1 cup honey.

Italian seasoning—1/4 teaspoon *each* of dried oregano leaves, dried marjoram leaves, and dried basil leaves plus 1/8 teaspoon rubbed dried sage can be substituted for 1 1/2 teaspoons Italian seasoning.

Ketchup—1 cup tomato sauce plus 1/2 cup sugar plus 2 tablespoons vinegar can be substituted for 1 cup of ketchup (for use in cooking).

Lemon—2–3 tablespoons lemon juice plus 1–2 teaspoons rind can be substituted for 1 medium lemon.

Marshmallows, miniature—10 large marshmallows can be substituted for 1 cup miniature marshmallows.

Mushrooms—6 ounces canned mushrooms can be substituted for 1 pound fresh mushrooms.

Mustard, dry—1 tablespoon prepared mustard can be substituted for 1 teaspoon dry mustard.

Mustard, prepared—1/2 teaspoon dry mustard plus 2 teaspoons vinegar can be substituted for 1 tablespoon prepared mustard.

Nutmeg, ground—1 teaspoon ground allspice ***or*** 1 teaspoon ground cloves ***or*** 1 teaspoon ground mace can be substituted for 1 teaspoon ground nutmeg.

Oats—Old-fashioned rolled oats and quick-cooking oats can be used interchangeably in baking recipes.

Oil—1 cup melted butter, margarine, or shortening can be substituted for 1 cup vegetable oil. Note: Recipe results may vary; texture and appearance may be affected.

Onion—1/4 cup instant minced onion or flaked onion ***or*** 1 teaspoon onion powder can be substituted for 1 cup chopped onion (1 medium onion).

Orange—6–8 tablespoons orange juice and 2–3 tablespoons grated rind can be substituted for 1 medium orange.

Poultry seasoning—1/4 teaspoon ground thyme plus 3/4 teaspoon ground sage can be substituted for 1 teaspoon poultry seasoning.

Pumpkin pie spice—1/2 teaspoon ground cinnamon plus 1/4 teaspoon ground ginger plus 1/8 teaspoon ground nutmeg plus 1/8 teaspoon ground cloves can be substituted for 1 teaspoon pumpkin pie spice.

Raisins—Substitute another chopped dried fruit for raisins. Golden raisins, dark raisins, and currants can be used interchangeably in baking recipes.

Salt—Kosher salt, iodized salt, sea salt, or a nonsodium salt substitute may be used for table salt in baking.

Shortening—1 cup butter or margarine can be substituted for 1 cup shortening. When using shortening in place of butter or margarine, you may need to add 1 tablespoon milk or water for each 1/2 cup shortening. Do *not* substitute vegetable oil for shortening when recipe calls for melting the shortening.

Sour cream—1 cup plain yogurt can be substituted for 1 cup sour cream.

Sugar, granulated—1 cup firmly packed brown sugar can be substituted for 1 cup granulated sugar. (Note: Flavor will be affected somewhat.) Or 3/4 cup honey can be substituted for 1 cup granulated sugar but reduce liquid in recipe by 1/4 cup.

Sugar, light brown—1/2 cup firmly packed dark brown sugar plus 1/2 cup granulated sugar can be substituted for 1 cup firmly packed light brown sugar. (Note: Slight flavor differences will occur.) Or 1 cup granulated sugar plus 2 tablespoons molasses can be substituted for 1 cup light brown sugar.

Tomatoes—1 (16-ounce) can of tomatoes can be substituted for 2 cups chopped fresh tomatoes.

Tomato sauce—3/4 cup tomato paste plus 1 cup water can be substituted for 1 cup tomato sauce.

Vanilla extract—Imitation vanilla flavoring can be substituted for vanilla extract. Other flavorings, such as almond, peppermint, rum, or lemon may be substituted for vanilla extract. (Note: Flavor differences will occur.)

Equivalent Measures

3 teaspoons	=	1 tablespoon
2 tablespoons	=	1/8 cup
4 tablespoons	=	1/4 cup
5 tablespoons plus 1 teaspoon	=	1/3 cup
8 tablespoons	=	1/2 cup
10 tablespoons plus 2 teaspoons	=	2/3 cup
12 tablespoons	=	3/4 cup
16 tablespoons	=	1 cup
2 tablespoons (liquid)	=	1 ounce
1 cup	=	8 fluid ounces
2 cups	=	1 pint (16 fluid ounces)
4 cups	=	1 quart
4 quarts	=	1 gallon

Apples—3 pounds of unsliced apples = 2 quarts of sliced

Bacon—8 slices fried = 1/2 cup crumbled

Cheese—1 pound = 4 1/2 cups shredded

Cottage Cheese—1 pound = 2 cups

Crumbs

- Bread: 4 slices = 1 cup fine crumbs
- Chocolate: 19 cookies = 1 cup crushed
- Graham crackers: 30–36 crackers = 3 cups crumbs
- Saltines: 28 crackers = 1 cup fine crumbs
- Vanilla wafers: 22 wafers = 1 cup fine crumbs

Dates, pitted—1 pound = 2 cups

Green pepper—1 pepper = 1 cup chopped

Herbs—1 tablespoon fresh = 1 teaspoon dried

Macaroni—2 cups uncooked = 4 cups cooked

Punch—12 quarts = 96 (4-ounce) punch glasses

Rice—1 cup raw = 3 to 3 1/2 cups cooked

Yeast—1 package = about 2 1/4 teaspoons

Favorite Hints

Cooking Bacon

When you need to cook a few pieces of bacon, try using a George Foreman grill. It's easy to do and grease drips into drainage cup.

Freezing Bananas

When you have brown or very ripe bananas, peel them and then freeze them in plastic wrap. I use them in breakfast drinks, frozen salads, and banana bread.

Making Buttered Breadcrumbs

Butter 1 side of white or wheat bread. Tear into pieces and grind in processor for several seconds. One slice bread = 1/2 cup crumbs.

Measuring Butter or Shortening

Before measuring butter or shortening, rinse the measuring cup with water. The butter or shortening will just slide out.

Cakes

I usually bake cakes ahead of time and freeze layers with plastic wrap between each layer. Frost them frozen on the day you want to serve. It makes frosting so much easier.

Cheese

Buying cheese in blocks is cheaper. Shred in food processor, store in plastic bags, label, and freeze.

Chicken

When cooking chicken for a casserole, always cook enough for several other casserole and soup recipes. Separate into the quantity for each recipe, label, and freeze in broth. This saves so much time.

Ground Chuck

When purchasing ground chuck for a specific dish, purchase 5 extra pounds. I always brown the meat, rinse it well, and then pulse it in a food processor for a finer texture. I divide the meat and label it for later use in tacos, spaghetti, casseroles, etc.

Toasting Coconut

Place 1 cup coconut on a microwaveable plate and microwave on high 3–4 minutes, stirring at 30-second intervals until lightly browned.

Rolling Cookie Dough

Sprinkle powdered sugar (instead of flour) on the surface to roll out cookie dough. It adds sweetness rather than excess flour.

Egg Whites

Leftover egg whites can be frozen for later use in another dish.

Fresh Fruit

Choose fruit according to taste and color. My favorite combination for a quick fruit salad or plate is cantaloupe, honeydew melon, pineapple, strawberries, blueberries, raspberries, and purple grapes. Garnish with kiwis.

When preparing brunch, you can cut some of the fruit the night before: cantaloupe, honeydew, and pineapple. Taste for sweetness; if not sweet enough, add a packet or two of sweetener. Store in separate plastic bags overnight in refrigerator, then add remaining fruit. For fruit that discolors easily, dip in lemon juice or clear carbonated soda.

Easy Greasing

To grease a pan without greasing your fingers, insert your hand into a plastic bag. Hold the butter or shortening in your bag-lined hand and spread it in the pan.

Lemons and Oranges

If you are eating oranges or using lemons for juice, always grate some of the rind for later use. Store in freezer. (Always label what you freeze.)

Planning a Party

When planning an open house or dinner party, select a couple of dishes that can be prepared ahead of time and frozen or refrigerated. Also, we are blessed to live in a time where you can purchase great prepared food. You must remember that the food is just a tool—the fellowship is what is important.

Index